PASSION

THE FRENCH IDEAL AND THE AMERICAN DREAM

FOR WINE

PASSION
THE FRENCH IDEAL AND THE AMERICAN DREAM
FOR WINE

JEAN-CHARLES BOISSET
& MARNIE OLD

 Favorite Recipes® Press

Contents

1 THE HISTORY OF WINE
FRENCH IDEAL; AMERICAN DREAM   14

2 THE FUNDAMENTALS OF WINE TASTING
DEVELOPING A SENSORY CHECKLIST   32

3 THE SOURCES OF WINE'S DIVERSITY
PREDICTING VARIATIONS IN FLAVOR

4 THE SPECTRUM OF STYLE
SORTING WINES BY HOW THEY TASTE

5

THE NOBLE GRAPE VARIETIES
WINE'S KEY INGREDIENTS
102

6

THE ART OF WINE LIVING
HOME ENTERTAINING & PAIRING WITH FOOD
124

7 THE MAGICAL WORLD OF BOISSET
VISITING FRENCH & AMERICAN WINE COUNTRY 140

APPENDIX—FRANCE & THE USA
WINE LABELS & WINE REGIONS 160

ABOUT THIS BOOK
AN INVITATION TO EXPLORE WINE WITH CONFIDENCE

Every chapter of this book is sure to surprise, illuminate, and delight, whether exploring these pages represents the first step on your wine journey or simply a new perspective on one of your most cherished passions. In merging our unique perspectives as a French vintner and an American *sommelièr*, our aim was not to boil wine down to its minutiae or production statistics. Instead, we chose to write the book that the wine world needs most: one that shares the compelling ideas, useful generalizations, and practical wine skills that separate the wine expert from the wine novice.

As a result, *Passion for Wine* charts an unusual path toward wine enlightenment. It makes use of the lessons of Franco-American history, the principles of sensory science, the power of visualization, and the reassuring constancy of Mother Nature's ways to make sense of wine. This refreshingly direct approach is as intellectually unconventional, sensually exciting, and visually stimulating as a glass of the finest French bubbles. While so many wine books drain the enjoyment out of wine by drowning the reader with data points, *Passion for Wine* is elegant in its simplicity, uplifting in its empowering message, and fearlessly honest in its embrace of the central truth behind wine's appeal: wine brings pleasure not only through the sum of its flavor, texture, and scent, but also in its extraordinary ability to elevate life's precious moments and strengthen the bonds of love and humanity that connect us all.

> "If you find wine to be delectable, transcendent, and captivating but also confusing, frustrating, or overwhelming, then fear not—*Passion for Wine* is the book for you."

Jeb   Mo

MEET JEAN-CHARLES BOISSET
A FRENCH VINTNER COMES TO AMERICA

As the famed French philosopher Brillat-Savarin first told us, it is true that we are what we eat. . . . And as importantly, we are what we drink as well! All that is palatable should be an exaltation, and no other drink is as divine, as illustrious, as alluring as wine. We breathe wine. We adore wine. For us, wine is not only a way of life; it is life! Wine enables us to cultivate a unique and genuine *art de vivre*. It is an infinite world of discovery, conviviality, generosity, and joy. Above all, wine is a passion meant to be shared.

Sommelièr extraordinaire Marnie Old and I wanted to transcend the bounds of a traditional wine book to bring exuberance and excitement to the way we share wine with the world. Wine is the most hedonistic, noble, and inspiring elixir that nature has created, and learning its mysteries and intricacies should be the same!

I was very fortunate to be born and raised in the world of wine in the village of Vougeot, in Burgundy, France, where my view was the vineyards of the world-renowned Château du Clos de Vougeot. Burgundy is the cradle of fine wine as we know it, the place where an agricultural crop began its ascension and transformation into one of the most sought-after, captivating, and sensual gifts of nature.

As a child, I played amidst vineyards that had been planted by Cistercian monks; my bedroom was literally above the barrel cellar and the winery. I was making wine from the very beginning. . . . At the age of eleven, I discovered the land of possibilities when I first visited California with my parents and grandparents. It was a *coup de foudre*—"love at first sight"! I was magnetized by the American dream, and I fell in love with the incredible history, heritage, authenticity, and freedom of Napa and Sonoma. Rooted in Burgundy with the spark of California, we invite you to discover the magic and power of wine's story, to master its intricacies, and—most of all—to create your own wine destiny. Find passion and *joie de vivre* in every bottle and every day!

Jean Charles Boisset

ABOUT JEAN-CHARLES BOISSET
Jean-Charles Boisset was born into the world of wine in the village of Vougeot in Burgundy, France. His parents, Jean-Claude and Claudine, founded the family winery in 1961 in one of the most traditional wine-growing regions in the world and with an innovative spirit. Today, the family collection includes wineries that share more than eighteen centuries of combined winemaking heritage in some of the world's most prestigious terroirs, from Burgundy and the south of France to California's Napa Valley and Russian River Valley. Jean-Charles leads the family firm with a passionate commitment to fine wine, history, and quality, and with a deep respect for the environment—he implemented organic and Biodynamic farming in all of the family's estate vineyards in Burgundy and California. Jean-Charles sets forth a vision of the wine world that is centered on family, passion, history, innovation, a commitment to fine wines, a dedication to sustainable wine growing, and a Franco-American spirit.

"Jean-Charles is an artist whose medium is passion, which is why I wanted to work with him. His infectious energy takes the stiffness out of wine and puts the *joie de vivre* back in."

MEET MARNIE OLD
AN AMERICAN SOMMELIER ON A MISSION

When I first became a wine professional, I noticed a strange disconnect. On the sensory level, wine's beauty is truly humbling and inspirational, with an appeal that is nearly universal. People love the way wine looks, how it smells, how it tastes, how it feels, and how it makes *them* feel. But on the intellectual level, wine's complexity can make it seem daunting. Between its arcane nomenclature and the sheer overwhelming number of wine options available, many newcomers find themselves discouraged. Even the well-informed can feel insecure.

I found it distressing to see so many wine drinkers unable to relax and enjoy wine's pleasures for fear of doing or saying (or drinking!) the wrong thing. I've set out to bridge this gap: to find ways to simplify wine and to make its charms more accessible to a wider audience without glossing over the remarkable intricacies that hold the key to our fascination with wine.

Luckily, I am not alone in this pursuit. I'm thrilled to be partnering with Jean-Charles Boisset on this project. He and I have very different communication styles—I'm a little bit *Sesame Street*, and he's a little more *Sex in the City*—but we're both singing the same tune. We love fine wines, of course, and the trappings of the wine life that can be a beautiful dream to share with others. But we recognize the need for everyday wines, too. The mark of true wine experts is that they have moved beyond the simple acquisition of wine knowledge toward a state of wine enlightenment, coming back full-circle to the same open-minded appreciation of pleasure that has led every wine novice to embark upon their journey of discovery. Armed with the confidence to make educated guesses based on a few central truths, wine insiders are able to relax and savor what's in the glass, whether it's a simple Chardonnay or a Grand Cru Burgundy.

What Jean-Charles and I aim to do in this book is provide a similar degree of comfort with wine for all wine drinkers. We invite you all—from well-traveled members of the connoisseur class to new initiates to the lore of wine—to join us for a riveting look at wine that will put you on the path to your own *vinlightenment* and *vindependence*!

Marnie Old

ABOUT MARNIE OLD

Marnie Old is a sommelier, wine author, and wine educator known for her insightful visual explanations of complex wine topics. She serves as an ambassador-at-large for the Boisset Collection, sharing her passion for wine as an expert speaker around the country and around the globe. She formerly served as the director of wine studies at New York's esteemed French Culinary Institute and as the founding education chairperson of the American Sommelier Association. Marnie's titles include the award-winning *Wine: A Tasting Course*, a revolutionary infographic introduction to wine, and the popular *He Said Beer, She Said Wine*, an entertaining debate on food pairing that she co-authored with Dogfish Head brewing legend Sam Calagione. In addition to her work as a wine educator, she reviews wines for the *Philadelphia Inquirer* and pens a humorous wine column for the *Philadelphia Daily News*.

> "Marnie brings vibrant energy and a dynamic approach to illuminating the world of wine. . . . She unites her extraordinary knowledge with appreciation for wine's pleasures, and inspires passion for the magical elixir we adore so much." *JeB*

THE HISTORY OF WINE
FRENCH IDEAL; AMERICAN DREAM

France is the birthplace of fine wine as we know it. Yes, wine may have originated elsewhere and other nations may rival her annual production, but France was the first to make truly great wines. Most of the world's top wines—especially those from New World regions like California—are still made in the image of French styles, using French grape varieties and French winemaking techniques. Why? The answer lies in the fascinating story of how our modern culture of fine wine came to be.

MAKING WINE FOR SURVIVAL
A DEFINING ACT OF CIVILIZATION

Winemaking predates recorded history. Alcohol is a product of fermentation. Fermentation is an early stage of spoilage in sugar-containing foods, like fruits, that can be manipulated to preserve these otherwise perishable goods. Since alcohol has antiseptic properties that inhibit microbiological organisms, fermentation historically created drinks that were healthful and nutritious alternatives to unsanitary water sources. Winemaking and beer brewing are key indicators that a particular group of humans have left nomadic life behind to form a "civilized" agricultural settlement.

The earliest archaeological evidence of an alcoholic drink is a crude Stone Age brew made roughly 9,000 years ago. Found in central China, it was fermented from a mash of grain, grapes, and honey. However, a wealth of Neolithic artifacts dating from 6000 BC to 4000 BC, which were found in what's now Georgia, Iran, and Armenia, suggest that pure-fruit wines in the modern sense were first produced in the region where eastern Europe and western Asia meet the Middle East (not far from Mt. Ararat).

Being the most suitable fruit for winemaking, grapes were among the earliest fruit crops to be domesticated, most likely in Georgia's Caucasus Mountains around 6000 BC. These cultivated wine grapes are now recognized as their own species, *vitis vinifera*, and remain responsible for almost all wine made today.

Wine was embraced and prized as a luxury by ancient civilizations for millennia, from the Sumerians and Babylonians in Mesopotamia to the Egyptians and Assyrians in the Levant. The seafaring Phoenicians spread wine grapevines from modern Lebanon throughout the Mediterranean basin, including the south of France. The ancient Greeks studiously refined the art of winemaking, meticulously recording their results. But it was not until the armies of Julius Caesar pushed north to claim Gaul for Rome in the first century BC that wine was introduced to what are now considered the classic wine regions of France, including Burgundy, the birthplace of fine wine as we know it.

6000 BC

Neolithic seeds of *vitis vinifera* found in southeastern Georgia are oldest known evidence of domesticated wine grapes.

5400 BC

Stone Age pottery shards from Zagros Mountains of Iran contain oldest known wine residue.

4100 BC

Copper Age Areni Caves in Armenia are home to the world's oldest known winery.

Until that point, grapevines grew mainly among the figs and olives of Mediterranean climates, where they thrive and produce copious amounts of fruit. When the Romans planted vineyards among the oak forests of continental France, however, the hot summers and harsh winters of this new temperate climate proved less hospitable. In challenging conditions where their survival is at stake, grapevines produce less fruit to conserve energy, so these northern vineyards undoubtedly yielded smaller crops than the southern norm. Yet Gaul's grapevines were not abandoned; indeed. their wines came to be traded throughout the Roman Empire, likely because reducing grape volume per vine improves wine quality, producing more concentrated wines that better resist spoilage.

" For millennia, wine has been at the epicenter of civilization . . . an essential actor of the table, and a catalyst for the development of human culture!" *JeB*

The famed Roman aqueduct Pont du Gard was constructed about 19 BC.

3100 BC	425 BC	52 BC
Bronze Age Palestinian wine jars found in Egyptian pharaoh's tomb provide earliest proof of large-scale wine importing and trading.	Iron Age Etruscan wine-press found in Languedoc is evidence of the earliest known winemaking in France.	First vineyards planted in France's Burgundy region by the Romans at Autun.

IMPROVING WINE WITH REVERENCE
THE KEY ROLES OF BURGUNDY & THE CLOS DE VOUGEOT

Prior to the medieval era, wine was already considered superior to beer, but its modern role as a luxury good is a direct result of its symbolic and ritual importance to Christian monks in the Middle Ages: red wine was transformed into the blood of Christ at the Last Supper, a practice reenacted in the Catholic rite of Communion. This exalted role in the New Testament gave wine an elite status unlike that of any other agricultural product.

Catholic monasteries were not simply large settlements that needed to make wine for sustenance and to celebrate their Mass. They also had incredible resources to invest in improving their wine, namely land, labor, and time. Since they recorded their successes and failures, they were able to learn from trial and error, sharing the resulting wisdom among their orders' monasteries and down through the generations.

For landowners and peasants, sacrificing crop volume to improve quality had never been practical. However, making better wine wasn't simply about efficiency for religious orders—it was a form of devotion to their faith. Improving wine also improved the status of an order or monastery since superior wines were viewed as a sign of divine favor by kings and popes alike. Beginning in the twelfth century in what is now central France, monasteries in Burgundy helped to transform wine from a rustic dietary staple into something sacred: a transcendent drink that both honored and symbolized the divine.

> Fine wine was born in the vineyards tended by Cistercian monks in Burgundy, the most famous of which is just a few hundred feet from my childhood home; their practices continue to inspire winemakers today."
>
> JeB

The Benedictines were followers of St. Benedict of Nurcia (left). The Cistercians were followers of St. Bernard de Clairvaux (right).

THE CISTERCIAN CRADLE OF FINE WINE

Devout communities of monks were formed in the final years of the Roman Empire and thrived in western Europe after its fall. Two of the most powerful were the Benedictine Abbey of Cluny and the Cistercian Abbey of Cîteaux, both located in what was then the Duchy of Burgundy. Cluny was founded in 910, and by the mid-twelfth century, it led a network of nearly 1,000 "Cluniac" monasteries of great wealth and political influence. These monasteries came to be known for their patronage of art and music. When Cîteaux was founded in 1098, it was as both an offshoot of the Cluniacs and a rebuke to them—the Cistercian Abbey of Cîteaux renounced wealth and returned to more ascetic principles, working the land to sustain its communities.

Under their charismatic leader St. Bernard of Clairvaux, the original Cistercian Abbey spawned over 500 "daughter houses" in its first century. Many of the methods used to improve wine quality today were developed or refined by the Cistercians of Burgundy and spread throughout France and Europe with the growth of their religious order. Cistercians were the first to use terms like *terroir* and *cru* to denote the unique flavor of a particular vineyard's wine and to recognize its superiority.

The very first vineyard established by the founding Cistercian monastery of Cîteaux was the Clos de Vougeot, a vineyard now recognized with its own Grand Cru appellation status as one of the world's finest sites for Pinot Noir. Begun with a gift of land in 1109 and completed in 1336, this walled vineyard in the heart of Burgundy's Côte de Nuits was located eight miles from the abbey. In many ways, the Clos de Vougeot is ground zero for fine wine as we know it today.

Above: Detail of an illuminated manuscript showing a Cistercian monk sampling wine from a barrel (Régime du Corps by Aldebrandin de Sienne, 1275).

Below: The historic Château de Clos de Vougeot, located in the heart of the Côte de Nuits. Some of the world's finest Pinot Noir wines continue to be grown in this vineyard to this day.

CULTIVATING WINE FOR COMMERCE
FRANCE LEADS THE WAY

The fame of Burgundy's excellent wines had a significant impact on the secular world that lay outside the monasteries. Having been the favorite wines of a succession of French popes, the wines of Beaune in particular became sought-after luxury goods among Europe's nobility. As the largest town in what is now the Côte d'Or, Beaune came to be the hub of trade in Burgundy wines, which were widely regarded as the world's finest.

When the Duchy of Burgundy was gifted to the king of France's youngest son in 1363 for him to rule as an independent state, wine was already the main driver of its economy despite the difficulty of transporting wine over land to key markets. At this time, under English rule, the wines of Bordeaux were widely traded; their fortunate proximity to a major port granted easy access to prosperous states outside of grape-growing areas. However, like most regions, the winemaking focus in Bordeaux was on quantity, not (yet) on quality. In contrast, sacrificing volume to improve quality was essential in landlocked Burgundy, and not simply as a religious duty—only the best-made wines could withstand long journeys by cart or justify such an expense. In this spirit, Duke Philippe the Bold issued a proclamation in 1395 mandating that only Pinot Noir could be cultivated in his territory. He railed against the more prolific and economical Gamay grape as "very bad and very disloyal." This was the world's first law specifying which grape varieties were permitted in a given region, a concept that is now a core principle of modern European wine regulations.

Burgundy was eventually absorbed into France in 1477. Over the next few centuries, commerce came to rival both religion and noble families in shaping the nation. During this period, the wines of the great *crus* of Burgundy remained unrivaled in quality and reputation, despite their tiny volume.

THE RISE OF FRENCH WINE MERCHANTS

The story of Bouchard Aîné & Fils is useful as a lens through which to understand wine's commercialization in France. When Michel Bouchard moved his business to Beaune in 1731, it was to secure his future in the cloth trade. Sending Burgundy wines to his clients along with textiles likely began as a courtesy, but when Michel's son Joseph Bouchard took control of the business in 1750, the company became wine brokers in earnest. Within forty years, the wine trade had completely displaced the family's original cloth business. A 1776 edict eliminating local tariffs on wine within France caused a surge in demand for Burgundian wines, which in turn led Joseph to begin investing in vineyard land to secure additional stocks of wine. When the vineyard holdings of the church and nobility were nationalized and sold off after the French Revolution, the family firm was well-positioned to capitalize on that action by acquiring more vineyards at low cost (as were many others).

> "Founded in 1750, Bouchard Aîné & Fils pioneered the wine trade in Burgundy, supplying their European clients with the fine wines of the region. It is a pillar of tradition and a pinnacle of style!" *JeB*

The political and economic turbulence of the century that followed proved challenging, but it was also ripe with commercial opportunities. The wars that raged at the turn of the nineteenth century gave Burgundy an advantage over Bordeaux, which lost its access to British colonies and transatlantic trade. In addition, the daily rations of wine given to soldiers broadened the drink's audience. The advent of railway transport in the 1850s and Napoleon III's international free-trade treaty of 1860 allowed the Bouchards to expand their wine business well beyond France. By 1882, they were among the most influential families of Beaune; Paul Bouchard served as its mayor. In this capacity, he founded the School of Viticulture in Beaune that exists to this day, continuing the Burgundian legacy of the Cistercian monks and the Valois Dukes of Burgundy: to pursue quality over quantity.

Left: The Hospices de Beaune, founded in 1443, continues to play a central role in the Burgundy wine trade through its annual charity auction.

Right: Joseph Bouchard, founder of Bouchard Aîné & Fils 1720–1804

FINE WINE IN THE OLD WORLD
THE KEY WINE REGIONS OF FRANCE & EUROPE

Burgundian vintners were the first to systematically pursue quality over quantity on a grand scale. Their methods spread first to the other wine regions of France, as these were forced to compete with Burgundy's exceptional wines. As a result, French wines had such a significant head start that they faced no significant rivals in quality terms until the twentieth century. Even in other European countries that grow their own native grape varieties, the best wines are generally made using French techniques and are aged in French oak barrels. By the time winemaking rules were standardized throughout the European Union, the Burgundian system was adopted for all: naming wines for their place of origin, regulating permitted grape varieties, and establishing formal hierarchies based on wine quality.

FRANCE
Roughly the size of Texas, France is the world's wine leader in many ways. France's wine production is the highest in total volume by a nose and the highest in dollar value by a mile.

The wines of France's top seven regions also serve as archetypes for a significant proportion of the world's finest wines—in fact, their vine varieties are often described as "international grapes" because they are so widely cultivated outside their native France.

BURGUNDY: Chardonnay, Pinot Noir

CHAMPAGNE: Chardonnay, Pinot Noir, Pinot Meunier

BORDEAUX: Cabernet Sauvignon, Merlot, Malbec, Sauvignon Blanc, Cabernet Franc, Petit Verdot

RHÔNE VALLEY: Grenache (a.k.a. Garnacha), Syrah (a.k.a. Shiraz), Viognier

BEAUJOLAIS: Gamay

LOIRE VALLEY: Sauvignon Blanc, Chenin Blanc, Cabernet Franc

ALSACE: Pinot Gris (a.k.a. Pinot Grigio), Riesling, Pinot Blanc, Gewurztraminer

PORTUGAL
Portugal is best known for its blended wines, most particularly its liqueur-like fortified wines, such as Port, Madeira, and Moscatel.

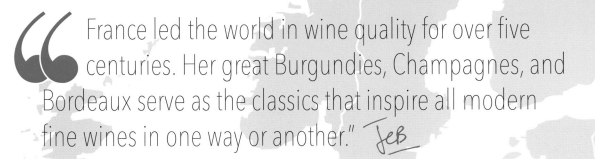

"France led the world in wine quality for over five centuries. Her great Burgundies, Champagnes, and Bordeaux serve as the classics that inspire all modern fine wines in one way or another." *JeB*

GERMANY

Vines can only thrive in the southwestern regions of Germany, most notably in the valleys of the Rhine and Mosel rivers. A single cold-hardy grape, the noble Riesling, dominates fine German wines. German white wines were the only significant rivals to French wines in quality or price before the twentieth century.

AUSTRIA

Since its western reaches are too mountainous for cultivating grapes, almost all Austrian wines are made in the east and much depends on a single vine variety, the brisk white Grüner Veltliner.

ITALY

Italy has more native *vitis vinifera* vines than any other nation; the most widely planted is the Tuscan Sangiovese grape. Italy also rivals France in total production, despite being smaller in size than the state of California.

SPAIN

Spain comes in a close third behind France and Italy in both total wine production and wealth of native grapes. Of these, red Tempranillo and white Albariño are most renowned.

GREECE

Greece is carpeted with its own native vines, but many of its grapes are dried into raisins. The region's wines have only recently come to the attention of international audiences.

FINE WINE IN THE NEW WORLD
THE AMERICAS & THE SOUTHERN HEMISPHERE

During the age of exploration, European colonists brought more than just their language and culture to the western and southern hemispheres (known collectively as the New World): along with their crops and their livestock, they planted their grapes to make wine. Most vineyards were planted in warmer, drier territory than Europe's wine lands, but irrigating these arid zones allowed pioneering vintners to avoid the risks of bad weather and lost crops. Generally speaking, the vines planted were the most productive "workhorse" varieties, like Zinfandel and Shiraz.

At first, only rudimentary wines were made in the colonies, but today, a number of New World nations produce exceptional wine. Learning their wine geography is less essential than it is for Europe, though, since New World appellations tend to be fewer in number, larger in area, and less complicated in regulatory terms. Navigating their labels is also easier because most New World wines are labeled by grape, and in the absence of Europe's proliferation of native grape varieties, a much smaller number of grapes are grown, most of which are French in origin.

AUSTRALIA
FIRST PLANTED: 1788

The vineyard regions "down under" tend to be warmer and drier than the global norm, but all hug the nation's cooler southern coastline. The most widespread grape, Shiraz, is none other than the Syrah of the Rhône, followed closely by Burgundy's Chardonnay.

SOUTH AFRICA
FIRST PLANTED: 1659

Only the southernmost region known as the Western Cape is cool enough to support fine wine grapes. It was among the first New World areas to rival Europe in wine quality. The Loire's Chenin Blanc and Rhône's Grenache and Syrah are widely planted, along with Chardonnay and Cabernet Sauvignon.

NEW ZEALAND
FIRST PLANTED: 1819

This latecomer to the grape-growing trade serves as a cool-climate exception to the warmer New World rule since it is so far from the equator and is surrounded by frigid ocean waters. Grapes that thrive in colder weather dominate plantings, such as the Loire's Sauvignon Blanc and Burgundy's Chardonnay and Pinot Noir.

UNITED STATES OF AMERICA
FIRST PLANTED: 1562

European vines did not immediately thrive in North America; they were thwarted by a local insect pest. Today, however, the United States is the world's fourth-largest wine producer and the largest outside Europe.

While there are wineries in all fifty states, over 95% of American wines are made on the West Coast and roughly 85% of the total come from a single state: California. The workhorse Zinfandel grape of Croatian origin was the most widely planted until it was recently supplanted by Bordeaux's Cabernet Sauvignon, with Chardonnay being the most popular white grape.

The only significant sources of fine American wines outside California are in the Pacific Northwest, where Washington favors Cabernet Sauvignon and Chardonnay and Oregon specializes in grapes of Burgundian origin, namely Pinot Noir and Pinot Gris.

CHILE
FIRST PLANTED: 1555

Chile's vineyards are in coastal valleys that are quite sunny and warm but which benefit from the cooling influence of the Pacific. The most-planted grapes are Bordeaux reds Cabernet Sauvignon and Merlot as well as Chardonnay.

ARGENTINA
FIRST PLANTED: 1551

Most Argentine vineyards are on the sunny, arid high plains and foothills that flank the Andes Mountains. The most planted grape is Malbec (from Bordeaux) along with the lighter Bonarda (recently identified as a French grape from alpine Savoie).

> Wines from New World regions tend to be made with French grapes, but most have a fruitier flavor profile than their archetypes, thanks to warmer climates and innovative winemaking less bound by tradition." *JeB*

PIONEERING WINE IN CALIFORNIA
FROM SPANISH MISSIONS TO SONOMA'S OLDEST WINERY

European vines adapted reasonably well to the southern hemisphere, but growing grapes in North America proved problematic. While American grape species were bountiful in the English and French colonies, their fruit made unpalatable wine, and attempts to cultivate the wine-friendly *vitis vinifera* species from Europe failed miserably. Only the Spaniards were able to establish vineyards of European grapes in what is now Mexico. Their plantings of the red "Misionero" variety (used for sacramental wine in Catholic missions) eventually reached the West Coast in 1689.

When Spain pushed north to claim what was then called Alta California in the eighteenth century, the Mission San Diego del Alcalá was its first settlement. California's first sustained vineyard was planted there in 1779, with the same "Mission" grape, a red *vinifera* variety of Spanish

> "Modern American winemaking began at Buena Vista Winery in 1857, where its founder pioneered the use of European varietals, insisted on quality-minded techniques, and constructed California's first stone winery and wine caves." *JeB*

origin that would dominate California's wines for the next hundred years. By the time Mexico declared independence from Spain in 1821, twenty more Missions had been founded along California's coast, each with its own vineyard. The annexation of California by the United States in 1846 (as well as California's Gold Rush) brought more settlers to a region where grapes were already a significant crop.

Left: Historical marker at the original Buena Vista Winery

Right: The original stone winery building at Buena Vista

THE LEGENDARY "COUNT OF BUENA VISTA"

When Agoston Haraszthy founded Buena Vista Winery in 1857, he was only 44 years old but had already lived a remarkable life. Born to a noble family in Hungary (where he learned the wine trade), he served as a bodyguard to Austrian royalty and as a legal magistrate before immigrating to the United States in 1842. He settled in Wisconsin, where he was dubbed "Count Haraszthy" and where he operated the first steamboat on the Mississippi before relocating to San Diego in 1849. There, he became the town's first sheriff and built its first jail.

With the Gold Rush making fortunes in Northern California, Haraszthy moved once again, this time to San Francisco, where he was appointed assayer at the new U.S. Mint. Throughout his American adventures, Haraszthy had planted wine grapes with little success. However, he was certain that the coastal valleys of Northern California would be suitable for vineyards.

In 1856, based on the promising wines of a small dry-farmed vineyard on the property, Haraszthy purchased the 800-acre Buena Vista Ranch near the town of Sonoma. He proceeded to build what is now California's oldest commercial winery and to dig its first wine caves. He pioneered Burgundian-style methods for improving wine, like planting vineyards on hillsides, farming without irrigation, and limiting crop yields to boost quality. His writings on wine growing became essential resources for the state's budding wine industry.

In 1861, Haraszthy obtained a commission from California's governor to study and report on how to best "promote the improvement and culture of the grapevine in California." He spent months touring Europe's fine wine regions, including Burgundy, Bordeaux, and Champagne, and returned home with thousands of grapevine cuttings from over 400 varieties of *vitis vinifera* with which to improve California's vineyards.

Haraszthy's story ended as colorfully as it began when Buena Vista's vineyard was the first in California to be fatally afflicted by the insect pest phylloxera. Bankrupted by its failure, the ever-enterprising Hungarian tried to start over with a sugar plantation in Nicaragua, only to be killed by alligators on the property in 1879.

Buena Vista founder Agoston Haraszthy

WINE IN THE NINETEENTH CENTURY
WINEMAKING ADVANCES & VITICULTURAL SETBACKS

In 1864, winemaking was revolutionized overnight when Louis Pasteur discovered that the mechanism for fermentation was yeast, a single-celled organism in the fungus family, whose role had previously been unknown (due to its microscopic size). This insight gave vintners greater control over the process and its results. Unfortunately, this extraordinary leap forward in the scientific knowledge of wine coincided with an agricultural disaster that would soon bring the entire wine world to its knees.

Phylloxera vastatrix is a tiny aphid-like insect native to North America that feeds on grapevine roots and leaves. American vine species had developed a natural resistance to phylloxera, but its venom was fatal to European vines. Indeed, this insect was the reason European grapevines had so consistently failed in America's English- and French-speaking colonies.

> " At the very moment that science unlocked the secrets of winemaking, a vineyard plague unlike any the world had seen before was unleashed." *Jeb*

Louis Pasteur

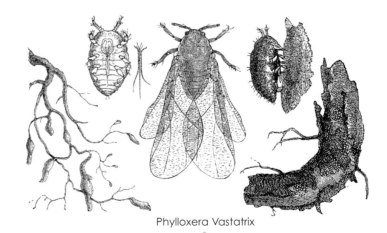

Phylloxera Vastatrix

1860s

In 1863, the first French vineyards are blighted. The following year, phylloxera is identified as the cause, and Louis Pasteur proves that yeasts produce alcohol via fermentation.

1870s

In 1875, French botanist Jules Émile Planchon begins grafting European vines onto native American vine roots to confer phylloxera resistance. This method succeeds and remains the only known solution to this day.

1880s

Fearing an impact on wine flavor, French vintners resist calls to graft their vines onto American roots, delaying France's recovery from the crisis.

When Agoston Haraszthy first noted the withering of his California vines at Buena Vista in 1860, he could not have known that the culprit was this soil-dwelling insect pest, nor could he have known that it had already been unwittingly introduced to Europe. At that very moment, phylloxera was infecting the vineyards of France, causing what would later come to be known as the Great French Wine Blight.

Phylloxera had crossed the Atlantic in the 1850s and spread like wildfire, triggering an unprecedented wave of vineyard devastation. By its height in the 1880s, phylloxera had nearly halved French wine production, and while France was hit first and hardest, other nations were not spared. An estimated 75% of European vineyards are thought to have succumbed to phylloxera between 1860 and 1900; eventually, phylloxera also found its way to the vineyards of South America, Australia, and Africa.

A solution was eventually found: grafting European vines like Chardonnay and Pinot Noir onto the roots of native American grapevine species could protect wine quality while bringing phylloxera under control, a protective measure practiced worldwide to this day. But the crisis had changed the wine world in a number of ways. While France had once ruled supreme, with no significant challengers in the realm of fine wine, the Great French Wine Blight had empowered her challengers in the New World and irrevocably altered the global wine economy.

In Montpellier, this monument honors Jules Émile Planchon and the role played by "the American vine" in resuscitating the vineyards of France.

1890s

Declining supply leads French wine prices to spike dramatically, creating an incentive to "fake" fine French wines and to source wines from the New World.

1900s

As crude fakes from Algeria are passed off as fine wines, French vintners riot in 1907, protesting cheap imports and rampant fraud.

WINE IN THE TWENTIETH CENTURY
FROM PROHIBITION TO THE FINE WINE REVOLUTION

Europe's wine shortage in the late nineteenth century led New World regions to swiftly increase production and provided an urgent need to improve their wine quality. By 1900, California wines made with fine French grape varieties (imported by Count Haraszthy) were earning international awards and acclaim.

However, just as California's star was on the rise, North America's anti-alcohol "temperance movement" was threatening its progress. Passage of the Eighteenth Amendment in 1919 slammed the door on the budding American wine industry by prohibiting the production of alcoholic drinks at the federal level. By the time Prohibition was repealed in 1933, 80% of California's wineries were defunct—many vineyards had been ripped out or replanted to grow table grapes.

World Wars I and II were major disruptions to the European wine trade, which had already been destabilized by phylloxera. Prohibition was an even more dramatic setback for American vintners, though—recovery took decades. At first, the priority was to restore production volume and maximize efficiency for simple, everyday wines. The agricultural school at the University of California–Davis pioneered and promoted techniques designed to boost crop yields and improve winery hygiene. During this period, modern methods of irrigation, mechanization, and chemical farming were widely embraced.

A policeman looks on as a barrel of beer is destroyed during Prohibition in the United States.

1920s

After Prohibition is enacted in the U.S. in 1919, American wineries are shuttered by the Eighteenth Amendment in 1920.

1930s

In 1933, the Twenty-First Amendment repeals Prohibition, but only a handful of California's wineries remain in business.

1940s

In 1944, the University of California–Davis publishes a climate map proposing which fine wine grapes to plant where.

> "Until the 1970s, French wines faced no real competition in fine wine. Today, California and other regions stand as equals in a truly diverse, and yet united, world of wine." *Jeb*

The drive to make quality wines in California was thus delayed until the late twentieth century. Finally, in the 1960s and 1970s, a handful of visionary vintners revisited Count Haraszthy's dream of making fine wine in places like Sonoma and Napa Valley. In 1976, their wines stunned the world by famously beating some of France's best red Bordeaux and white Burgundy wines in a blind tasting known as the Judgment of Paris, proving that California's best efforts could rival their French archetypes in quality.

In many ways, this upset sparked the global fine wine revolution and the diversification of the great wines we now enjoy. In recent decades, a confluence of advances in winemaking, communications, technology, and transportation have created what is truly a new golden age for wine lovers. But whether your taste preferences run more to the Old World or the New World, France and California remain the leaders in wine quality.

| 1950s | 1960s | 1970s | 1980s | 1990s | 2000s |

In 1966, Robert Mondavi founds the first new winery in Napa Valley since Prohibition. Mondavi focuses on making fine wines from fine French grape varieties and on promoting California's quality potential to Americans.

In the 1976 Judgment of Paris blind tasting, French experts rank California wines above top Bordeaux and Burgundy wines, proving the New World can compete on quality terms.

Boisset—by then one of the leading wine companies in Burgundy—acquires its first California winery in 1991, cementing the firm's commitment to a Franco-American future.

CHAPTER 2

THE FUNDAMENTALS OF WINE TASTING
DEVELOPING A SENSORY CHECKLIST

Wine is extraordinary but it has a serious communication problem—we don't always know how to talk about it. Fortunately, navigating the wine world becomes easier when we know what to look for as we taste and how to describe the variations in different styles of wine. There is no need to adopt pretentious lingo or to master expert-level minutiae, because, by using a simple sensory checklist, wine's most fundamental qualities can be assessed one sense at a time, enabling us to evaluate each new wine and describe the traits we most enjoy.

HOW TO TASTE WINE LIKE A PRO
ADOPT A CONSISTENT TASTING ROUTINE

Tasting wine the same way each time establishes a baseline we can use to compare our past and future wine experiences. The steps described below are designed to isolate and amplify the impact of wine's sensory characteristics: its colors, scents, flavors, and tactile mouthfeel. The goal is to make it easier to distinguish one wine from another and to recall which traits we enjoy or prefer to avoid.

HOW TO TASTE WINE

1 LOOK AT THE WINE

What color is it? Can you see bubbles or other clues as to how it might taste?

If the environment is well-lit, tilting the glass over a white surface (like a napkin) can yield more insights. How deep is the wine's color? Is it showing the signs of browning that might indicate age?

2 SWIRL THE WINE

We swirl glasses to intensify the smell of wine, a bit like turning up the volume on a radio.

Swirling wine increases its surface area and therefore boosts the rate of evaporation of its aroma compounds. These are then trapped and concentrated in the bowl of the wine glass, which makes them easier for us to detect.

3 SNIFF THE WINE

Dip your nose into the wine glass and take two or three deep sniffs.

Think about what you are smelling. How intense is the aroma? Does it remind you of anything? Fruits or vegetables? Herbs or spices? Do you smell toasty oak barrels? Smell is the main source of pleasure in wine tasting, so take your time.

> "Wine tastes amazing no matter how you drink it. . . .
> But if you want to develop your own wine voice, it helps
> to follow the same steps each time you taste a new wine." *Jeb*

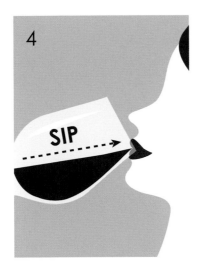

4 SIP THE WINE

Take a slightly larger sip than you normally would at dinner, but don't swallow right away.

It's illuminating to hold the wine in the mouth a little longer as we take the next step—say, for three to five seconds. This is another fun part, so be sure to enjoy it.

5 SWISH THE WINE

Before you swallow, swish the wine around in your mouth, treating it almost as if it were mouthwash.

Taking this step increases our surface of contact with the wine and also warms it with body heat, speeding its rate of evaporation. Both factors dramatically amplify our sensory perceptions of taste, smell, and tactile mouthfeel.

6 SAVOR THE WINE

Take a moment to mentally tick through a sensory checklist of primary wine traits.

Wine's flavor does not disappear immediately—its aftertaste lingers for a minute or more, allowing you to assess its sensory qualities and make more personal judgments. For example, decide now whether or not you like the wine.

ANALYZING THE TASTING EXPERIENCE
USING LANGUAGE TO CRACK THE WINE CODE

Most wines look broadly similar, but almost all of the pleasure we take in them comes from how wine tastes, smells, and feels in the mouth. Sadly, there are far fewer words for flavors, scents, and textures than there are for sights and sounds. Even with these limitations, however, describing our perceptions of wine is the single best way to build expertise, because if we don't capture those percep-

> "To enjoy a glass of wine requires no prior knowledge, but with the right words we can express its magic." *JeB*

tions in words, wine's fleeting sensations fade quickly. At the same time, our words needn't be technical or precise. Maybe a sparkling wine reminds you of Tinkerbell's fairy dust or seems full of the vibrato of violins. The terms you use don't matter; in fact, the most personal descriptions provide the most vivid recall.

That said, wine professionals need to communicate with one another, so they've had to develop language to describe wine that can be more universally understood. They do this by using descriptors that fall into two broad categories that we'll call "direct" and "indirect."

Indirect descriptions are those we most often see in wine reviews or hear at wine tastings. These are metaphors that compare a wine to something more familiar. Since there are so few words for smells, tastes, and textures, saying that a wine is "peppery" or "velvety" communicates a complex idea in a single word. This type of language is great for making nuanced distinctions between wines, but it can be intimidating for newcomers. Indirect language is more advanced; however, it comes to us naturally as we gain wine experience and the confidence that comes with it.

Direct wine language is a better place to start because it uses terms with fixed meanings to assess very specific wine characteristics on a more or less linear scale. There are very few direct terms, but they are the wine equivalent of the ABCs: words like "dry" or "oaky" or "tannic." Direct language is simpler to learn and more broadly useful for the beginner, so that's where we'll begin.

FRENCH
BOURGOGNE CHARDONNAY
DESCRIPTORS

DIRECT	INDIRECT
White	Straw-Gold
Tart	Green Apple
Unoaked	Mineral
Lightweight	Vivacious

NAPA VALLEY
CABERNET SAUVIGNON
DESCRIPTORS

DIRECT	INDIRECT
Dark	Garnet
Dry	Chocolaty
Oaky	Velvety
Tannic	Powerful

A SENSORY CHECKLIST
FOR WINE'S MOST TANGIBLE TRAITS

Following a consistent wine-tasting technique allows us to to make use of the final step: pausing for a moment to savor the wine to assess a series of objective wine characteristics using "direct" language. Think of each new wine you taste as a new entry in a mental database. Deciding how it compares to others you've tried determines where it's entered.

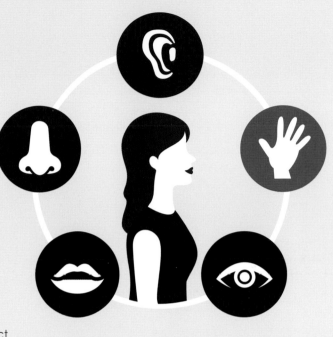

1 SIGHT
The most obvious differences between wines are the differences we can see, so much so that red, white, and pink (or rosé) are the most fundamental of all wine classifications.

2 TASTE
The word "taste" is used informally for all sensations in food and drink, but there are technically only two things in wine that the tongue can detect on contact and taste alone: sweetness and acidity.

3 SMELL
Most of what we call "flavor" is not a taste but a smell. While wine flavors are very diverse, they come from only two sources: from fruit or from the use of new oak barrels.

4 TOUCH
We don't think of touch as having a role in tasting, but whether or not we enjoy a wine is often based on its tactile characteristics, which winemakers refer to as "mouthfeel."

		LOW	MEDIUM	HIGH
SIGHT	COLOR	White	Pink	Red
	COLOR DEPTH	Pale	Medium	Deep
TASTE	SWEETNESS	Dry	Lightly Sweet	Fully Sweet
	ACIDITY	Soft	Crisp	Tart
SMELL	FRUIT FLAVOR	Mild	Moderate	Bold
	OAK FLAVOR	No Oak	Toasty	Oaky
TOUCH	WEIGHT/BODY	Lightweight	Midweight	Heavyweight
	TANNIN (RED ONLY)	Silky	Velvety	Suede-Like

HOW WINE LOOKS
FINDING FLAVOR CLUES IN WHAT WE SEE IN THE GLASS

Wines can look as clear as water or as opaque as ink, and there is often a strong connection between a wine's combination of hue and color saturation and how it will taste.

COLOR

Unless we're tasting wine by moonlight, it's quite apparent which are white, which are red, and which fall somewhere in between. The two most common wine colors, white and red, are not simply different colors but are wholly separate wine categories. Whites and reds are made by different winemaking processes and usually from different grapes. Wines in the pink middle ground are far less common, comprising a third category known as "rosé." (The French word for pink is "rose," so a "rosé" wine is literally one that has been "pinked.")

> "They say we eat with our eyes, but we drink with our eyes as well. Wine's brilliance, clarity, and colors are worthy of a jeweler's setting." —JeB

WHITE WINES DARKEN WITH AGE ⟶   PINK/ROSÉ

COLOR	TERMS	DESCRIPTION	WINE EXAMPLE
LOW	WHITE	Transparent with a yellow hue, as with apple juice or white grape juice	Chardonnay
MEDIUM	PINK/ROSÉ	Transparent with a pink hue, as with a splash of cranberry juice in water or pink lemonade	Rosé of Pinot Noir
HIGH	RED	Transparent to opaque and with a red to violet hue, as with red grape or pomegranate juice	Merlot

COLOR DEPTH

Differences in color saturation register as a color shift in whites and rosés (shading from paler to more vivid hues) and as varying degrees of transparency or color saturation in reds. Many of the variables that affect a wine's flavor also change its depth of color. Some red grapes have thicker skins than others, yielding paler or darker color that tends to correlate with flavor intensity. High degrees of grape ripeness can also deepen grape color in warmer regions, resulting in bolder, spicier flavors. Fermenting white wines in charred oak barrels can darken their color, while color in rosé wines mostly depends on how much time the juice spends in contact with grape skins and at what temperature.

However, the depth of a wine's color is most useful as an indicator of its maturity. All wines oxidize over time, meaning that all will eventually die and turn brown. Oxidation slowly adds an amber cast (like the browning of a cut apple) and progresses much faster in porous wooden barrels than in inert glass bottles or steel tanks. White wines will always brown and grow darker with age, moving from white to yellow to gold to amber. Red wines shift from bluish red to yellowish red as they age, moving from inky violet to blood red to brick red to russet. But where whites get darker, reds will always grow paler over time because their color comes from a suspension of particles that eventually succumb to gravity and settle as sediment.

←——— RED WINES GROW PALER WITH AGE

COLOR DEPTH	TERMS	DESCRIPTION	WINE EXAMPLE
LOW	PALE	Very subtle coloration in whites and rosés, or completely translucent in reds	Pinot Grigio or Pinot Noir
MEDIUM	MODERATE	More color saturation in whites and rosés, or shading toward a core of opacity in reds	Chardonnay or Zinfandel
HIGH	DEEP	Vibrant color saturation in whites and rosés, or mostly opaque past the rim in reds	Sherry or Cabernet Sauvignon

WINE TASTING DECONSTRUCTED
THE THREE SENSORY DIMENSIONS OF "TASTE"

The word "taste" is used informally for all sensations that happen in the mouth, but when we analyze wine, we make distinctions between traits perceived by different senses, using separate terms for characteristics detected along three sensory pathways: taste, smell, and touch. For example, we might say that ice cream "tastes" sweet, creamy, and chocolaty in everyday speech. But from the sensory science perspective, only its sweetness is considered an actual taste because it alone is detected by the tongue's tastebuds. The chocolate we perceive as a "flavor" is really an olfactory sensation (or smell), while creaminess is a tactile sensation that falls under the category called "mouthfeel."

When it comes to wine, the word "taste" is routinely used in its informal sense—we "taste wine" and we attend "wine tastings." But when experts analyze how individual wines taste, we separate the three sensory strands that normally intertwine when we take a sip, distinguishing true tastes from smells and the physical sensations that comprise wine's mouthfeel. This is much easier to do once we understand how each sense operates.

TASTE	A narrow range of only six true "tastes" can be detected on contact with the tongue.
SMELL	Many thousands of scents can be discerned, but our brains tend to register those detected before tasting as odors and those perceived during or after tasting as flavors.
TOUCH	Mouthfeel traits like textures and tannins are perceived only on physical contact with the tongue.

THREE SENSES ARE ENGAGED WHEN WE "TASTE"

TASTE (mouthfeel)

SMELL

TOUCH

SWEETNESS · ACIDITY · UMAMI · SALTINESS · BITTERNESS · FAT

THERE ARE ONLY **SIX** THINGS WE CAN TASTE WITH THE TONGUE ALONE

Of all our senses, smell is the most important in the wine world. Even if we don't sniff our wine before tasting, we get an intense blast of smell every time we take a sip. Olfactory nerves in the nasal cavity detect aromas when we sniff, which are recognized as smells. But if the same scents reach these same olfactory nerves from the other direction (via the internal passage that connects our nose and mouth), we instinctively classify the perception differently and think of it as part of how food or drink "tastes."

> "Smell is the key sense of the wine-tasting experience, where wine's essence invades the body to deliver pleasure even before the first sip." *JeB*

We can taste only two rudimentary wine traits upon tongue contact: sweetness and acidity. We do, however, perceive many more complex characteristics when wine aromas reach our olfactory nerves. These initially register as smells when we sniff wine in the glass, then register again (with greater intensity) as flavors when we take a sip. This second blast of smell is amplified in two ways: by greater proximity to the source and by the increased evaporation rate as the volatile aroma compounds in the wine warm to body temperature. Smelling our food and drink before we take a bite or sip gives an accurate "preview" of how they will taste because so much of "taste" is not technically tasted but rather smelled.

BUT THERE ARE OVER **10,000** THINGS WE CAN SMELL THAT CAN REGISTER AS "FLAVORS"

NOT CONVINCED?
TAKE THE SMELL TEST

- Pour yourself a glass of any fruit juice
- With one hand, firmly plug your nose
- With the other, lift the glass and take a sip
- Swallow (awkwardly) and wait 5 seconds
- Release your nose to restore air flow

Note that without natural air flow, only the juice's sweetness and acidity are apparent. The distinctive fruit "flavors" do not register at all until the nasal passage is reopened. Why? Because they are not tastes, they are smells.

HOW WINE TASTES
THE LIMITED RANGE OF THE TONGUE

The tongue can only perceive six rudimentary sensations, always on contact with the taste buds. Four are quite apparent: sweetness, sourness (or acidity), saltiness, and bitterness. The others are less obvious: the barely detectable taste of fat and the broadly savory "umami" taste of amino acids like MSG. Taste buds are not evenly distributed on the tongue, but rather are concentrated around the edges and densest at the tip. Tongue sensitivity can also vary widely between individuals.

SWEETNESS

Sweetness is a sugary sensation, as found in candy or fruit. Most wines have no perceptible sweetness and are described as "dry." (This "dry" means "not wet"

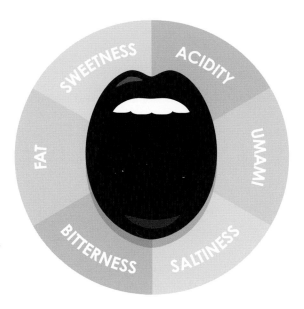

SWEETNESS	TERMS	DESCRIPTION	WINE EXAMPLE
LOW	DRY	No noticeable presence of sugar, as with unsweetened coffee	French Chablis
MEDIUM	LIGHTLY SWEET; OFF-DRY	Slight, noticeable presence of sugar, as with coffee with one spoonful of sugar	German Riesling
HIGH	SWEET	Obvious, strong presence of sugar, as with coffee with five spoonfuls of sugar	California Moscato

SWEETNESS
Sweetness is measured in grams of sugar per liter of wine (g/l), as shown below alongside other drinks.

DRY
PINOT NOIR

TEA
WITH ONE
SUGAR

ORANGE
JUICE

SWEET
PORT

WINE GRAPE
JUICE

2   12   85   100   255

> Among tastes, only sweetness and acidity are relevant in assessing wine, but both traits are absolutely essential for categorizing wine by style." *Jeb*

in everyday language, but when applied to wine or other drinks, dry always means "not sweet.") Historically, sweet wines were rare because dry wines are easier to make and resist spoilage. However, faint sweetness can be found in many modern wines, particularly in mass-market wines. Fully sweet wines or "dessert wines" are still quite rare because they are expensive to produce.

ACIDITY

Acidity is a sour sensation, as found in lemon juice. Wine grapes are very tart, so wines are more acidic than most drinks, which helps them flatter food and age gracefully. Since high levels of acidity can be an acquired taste, wine professionals tread carefully when choosing descriptors, avoiding negative terms like "sour" and "acidic" in favor of more appetizing terms like "tart," "crisp," or "refreshing."

ACIDITY	TERMS	DESCRIPTION	WINE EXAMPLE
LOW	MILDLY ACIDIC; FLABBY	Noticeable but mild degree of acidity, as found in baked apples or applesauce	Old Vine Zinfandel
MEDIUM	CRISP; TANGY	Standard, moderate degree of acidity, as found in red apples or apple juice	Napa Valley Cabernet Sauvignon
HIGH	TART; SHARP	Uncommonly strong degree of acidity, as found in green apples or apple cider	French Red Burgundy

ACIDITY

The pH scale measures acidity on a scale from 0 to 14, with 0 being the most acidic and 14 being the most alkaline. Water is ranked at a neutral point between acid and alkaline, at a pH of 7, while wine is quite acidic, in the 3 to 4 range of pH.

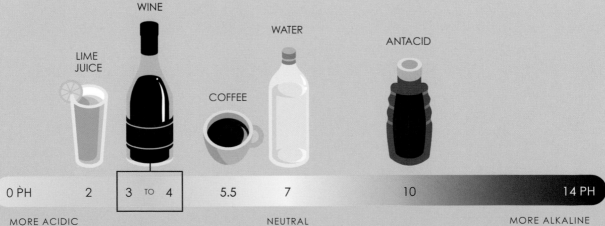

LIME JUICE — WINE — COFFEE — WATER — ANTACID

| 0 PH | 2 | 3 TO 4 | 5.5 | 7 | 10 | 14 PH |

MORE ACIDIC — NEUTRAL — MORE ALKALINE

HOW WINE SMELLS
THE NUANCED DISCERNMENT OF THE NOSE

Almost all of the pleasure we take from wine is olfactory, but playing "name that smell" is not the most useful way for beginners to analyze wine's scent. The average person can distinguish thousands of smells, but few could put a name to even a hundred of them. In addition, since smells are tied directly to memories and emotions, olfactory perception is highly subjective. It's true that wine professionals talk about wine in hyper-specific terms—they sketch out a wine's character indirectly by using comparisons that range from broad flavor families like "red berry" or "tropical fruit" to narrow aromas like "cedar" or "chocolate." However, it's often more productive for beginners to use simpler direct terms. Wine flavors derive from two main sources: grapes or oak barrels. The first step is to learn to distinguish these olfactory components—known as "fruit" and "oak"—and assess their intensity level.

FRUIT FLAVORS & SCENTS

Fruit is wine's primary olfactory component—it's always present, but the strength of it varies. Fruit is a catchall term for the totality of the scents and flavors in wine, derived from grapes or from the fermentation process. Simply put, everything you smell in wine that is NOT oak is part of its "fruit component."

FRUIT FLAVOR	TERMS	DESCRIPTION	WINE EXAMPLE
LOW	MILD; SUBTLE	Understated flavor, as found in herbal chamomile tea	Italian Pinot Grigio
MEDIUM	MODERATE; FLAVORFUL	Standard concentration of flavor, as found in strong black tea	French Pinot Noir
HIGH	BOLD; CONCENTRATED	Intense, powerful flavor, as found in espresso	California Petite Sirah

FRUIT: A CATCHALL TERM

It's important to note that wine's fruit component doesn't always smell like fruits per se—think of "fruit" as an umbrella term for a wide range of wine flavors and scents. It includes plenty of fruit-like flavors, such as the pineapple aroma of ripe Chardonnay or the pomegranate flavor of French Pinot Noir. But in wine lingo, non-fruit flavors are also considered part of the "fruit component" as long as their source is grapes or fermentation, so whether we're talking about a peppery flavor in Syrah, an herbal scent in Sauvignon Blanc, or a floral smell in Moscato, all of these flavors and scents would be considered part of a wine's fruit component.

OAK FLAVORS & SCENTS

Oak is a minor olfactory component. It's found only in wines seasoned with new oak, as with those that are either barrel-aged or barrel-fermented. Not all wines see oak treatment, and some that do, see only "neutral oak," i.e., older barrels that impart no oak flavor at all and whose wines, therefore, taste virtually "unoaked."

"If wine is art, it is art for the nose. No other sense can fully appreciate its layers of nuance and complexity." *JeB*

Oak has a distinctive range of flavors and smells that is very narrow compared to the exceptional range of wine's fruit component. In addition to smelling "woody" like lumber, new oak can add appetizing flavors like vanilla, dessert spices, coconut, toffee, pickling spices, or toasted nuts. Among woods, oak is known for its pleasing aromatics, which is why only oak barrels are used for flavoring whiskey and brandy.

OAK FLAVOR	TERMS	DESCRIPTION	WINE EXAMPLE
LOW	NO OAK; UNOAKED	Absence of oak flavor, as found in Vodka (either no barrels used or only neutral barrels)	California Sauvignon Blanc
MEDIUM	TOASTY; MILD OAK	Mild presence of oak scents and flavors, as found in young Irish Whiskey	French Meursault
HIGH	OAKY; BARREL-SPICED	Strong presence of oak scents and flavors, as found in fine, aged XO Cognac	Napa Valley Cabernet Sauvignon

OAK: THE WINEMAKER'S SEASONING

Oak barrels were first used in winemaking for purely practical purposes—historically, vats, casks, and barrels were the most common containers for all liquids, and oak was the tree whose wood made the best barrels. Nowadays, we still use barrels even though they are not as efficient as steel tanks, mostly because winemakers like to add oak flavor to wine.

Chefs can use herbs and spices to add flavor to their recipes, but wines must be made with 100% grape juice. Fermenting or aging wine in new oak barrels is the only way winemakers can add a different flavor to wine than the flavor that comes from the grapes. Oak qualities are eminently desirable in some styles, such as premium red wines and heavier whites, but are unwanted in others, like rosés and sparkling wines.

HOW WINE FEELS
THE PHYSICAL SENSATIONS KNOWN AS MOUTHFEEL

Some sensory aspects of how wine tastes are neither tastes nor smells but tactile sensations perceived on the tongue and palate. Many of our favorite food traits fall into the category known as "mouthfeel," such as the smooth texture of ice cream or the crunch of potato chips. In wine, we notice temperature and carbonation as physical sensations too, but for analyzing wine, we focus on the two tactile factors that help us classify wine by style. These are weight and tannin, also known as body and astringency.

WEIGHT

Wines are often described as lighter or heavier, lighter-bodied or fuller-bodied. These words reference wine's mouthfeel in terms of texture or thickness—essentially, its palpable viscosity. Just as sauces feel heavier when they contain more butter, wines feel heavier when they contain more alcohol. A few other factors can boost a wine's perceived weight, such as barrel-aging, lees-aging, or the high levels of sugar found in dessert wines. However, alcohol content is by far the most important. As a rule of thumb, midweight wines are those that contain 13% to 14% alcohol. Wines with lower alcohol will feel lighter and more sheer, while those with higher alcohol will feel heavier and richer.

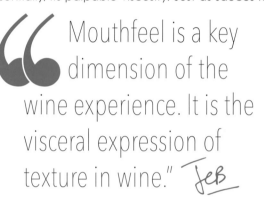

" Mouthfeel is a key dimension of the wine experience. It is the visceral expression of texture in wine." *JeB*

| CLOUD | FEATHER | SILK | CASHMERE | BUTTER | LEATHER |

WEIGHT/BODY	TERMS	DESCRIPTION	WINE EXAMPLE
LOW	LIGHTWEIGHT; LIGHT-BODIED	Sheer, delicate texture, as found in low-fat milk	Sparkling Wine
MEDIUM	MIDWEIGHT; MEDIUM-BODIED	Standard medium texture, as found in whole milk	French Pinot Noir
HIGH	HEAVYWEIGHT; FULL-BODIED	Rich, viscous texture, as found in cream	Napa Cabernet Sauvignon

TANNIN

Tannin causes the distinctive dry-mouth feeling that is associated with red wines but which is almost never found in other styles. Its effect can range from a subtle fuzzy feeling (like biting into a ripe peach) to a more assertive leathery feeling (as if someone had wallpapered the inside of your mouth with suede). Communicating about tannin is complicated by a quirk of wine language—even though high-tannin wines dry out the mouth moisture-wise, we don't call them "dry wines." As mentioned earlier, "dry" has a different meaning in wine lingo, namely the absence of sweetness.

Tannins are phenolic compounds that add color, flavor, and texture to wine. They come mainly from grape skins, though grape stems and oak barrels can also be minor contributors. We find significant tannin levels only in red wines because only reds are fermented in contact with grape skins. A red wine's tannin level largely reflects the tannin content of its grapes—mainly their variety and degree of ripeness—but is also strongly influenced by a winemaker's actions. Using thick-skinned grapes and techniques that maximize extraction of color and flavor tend to increase tannin, while using thinner-skinned grapes and techniques that minimize extraction of color and flavor tend to reduce tannin.

Tannin compounds are powerful antioxidants that preserve wine by slowing the oxidation that degrades them over time. Tannin often gets a bad rap because we notice it most when it's least pleasant. However, without tannin, red wines would lose their deep color, intense flavor, velvety texture, and ability to age. Tannin compounds also hold the key to the unique health benefits of red wine.

| FUR | ROSE PETAL | RIVER STONE | MOSS | WOOD | COCO HUSK |

TANNIN	TERMS	DESCRIPTION	WINE EXAMPLE
LOW	SILKY; LOW OR NO TANNIN	Barely detectable mouth-drying astringency, as found in mint tea	French Beaujolais
MEDIUM	VELVETY; SOFT TANNIN	Gentle mouth-drying astringency, as found in Earl Grey tea with milk	California Merlot
HIGH	SUEDE-LIKE; HARD TANNIN	Aggressive mouth-drying astringency, as found in strong green tea	Young California Cabernet Sauvignon

HOW TO ASSESS WINE
EVALUATING QUALITY & IDENTIFYING FAULTS

It's easy to tell if a wine "tastes good" according to one's own personal tastes, but learning how to recognize a "good wine"—meaning a wine that is well-made and has been kept in good condition—is one of the biggest challenges for newcomers to wine. While professionals look for many different clues, there are two simple skills anyone can learn that simplify these key value judgments: how to detect and evaluate a wine's finish and how to recognize indicators that a wine may be flawed by "cork taint."

FINISH

Of all quality indicators, a wine's "finish" or "length" is the most important, and, luckily, the easiest to discern. Both terms refer to the lasting impression of taste, smell, and mouthfeel that remains in the mouth after we've swallowed a sip of wine. The longer pleasant sensations last in the mouth, the more certain we can be that the wine is well-made and in pristine condition. Science has yet to explain why, but it is undeniably true that the finish is longest on wines made from the grapes of highest quality that are handled the most gently during winemaking and stored the most carefully. Therefore, assessing a wine's finish is a great way to tell if a wine is "good," even if we don't personally like the style.

Finish is also a terrific way to tell if wine has been damaged in shipping or storage, because exposure to heat or sunlight degrades and shortens a wine's finish. This helps explain why modest wines always taste

> "A wine's finish is not simply a lingering of its flavor and texture. It is a vibrational energy that resonates in the mouth after we take a sip." *JeB*

FINISH: A FANCY WORD FOR AFTERTASTE

Also known as "length," the lingering sensory impressions of a wine's finish can last for anywhere from 30 seconds to 5 minutes. How long the impressions persist is a direct reflection of the wine's quality and its condition.

It's useful to think of a wine's finish as if it were a sound that resonates before fading. The short finish on a modest wine would be like the clinking of two coffee cups—not an unpleasant sound but brief and shallow. The long finish of a premium wine would have a richer tone and last longer in a way that's more pleasing. Imagine the bell-like tone that happens when you clink two crystal wine glasses together. Truly great wines can reverberate on the palate far longer, holding without fading for minutes on end, like the uncanny note of a tuning fork hanging in the air.

best near their source—the farther they travel, the more likely it is that they will have sustained significant damage to their finish.

CORK TAINT

Wine bottles have been sealed with cork stoppers for centuries, but many vintners are now switching to cork-free packaging. Why? Since cork is a type of wood, it is porous and organic, not inert like glass. As such, it cannot be sterilized and can sometimes ruin wine flavor.

On average, 5% of cork-sealed wines are noticeably contaminated by their cork. Of these, the vast majority suffer from one specific problem called "cork taint" and are referred to as wines that are "corked." Sadly, the degree of damage from cork taint varies dramatically. In most cases, only a wine professional can identify the problem with certainty.

Technically, cork taint is a term used to describe the detectable effects of a chemical compound called trichloranisole 2-4-6, or TCA, for short. In the worst cases, TCA gives off a characteristic mildew scent, like that of a moist and moldy basement. In such cases, most people can recognize that the wine is "off."

TCA is much more insidious in mild cases, though, at which times it can be more apparent from the absence of good wine smells than from the presence of bad ones. Even at very low concentrations, TCA can interfere with our ability to detect wine's fruit, the very olfactory flavors and scents that we most enjoy in wine. It's very difficult to recognize these low concentrations unless you do a side-by-side comparison of more than one bottle of the same wine. The wine trade is well aware of the cork taint issue, which helps explain why more and more wines are going cork-free.

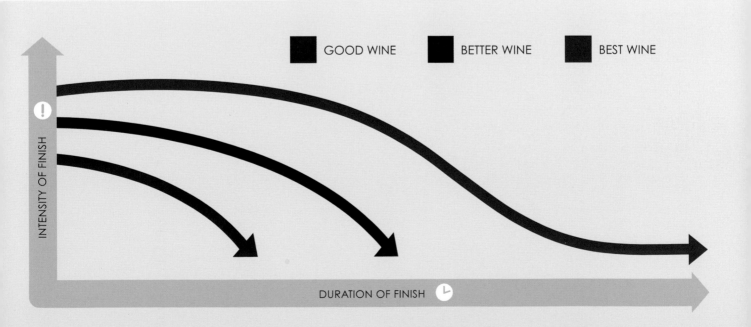

GOOD WINE   BETTER WINE   BEST WINE

INTENSITY OF FINISH

DURATION OF FINISH

THE SOURCES
OF WINE'S DIVERSITY
PREDICTING VARIATIONS IN FLAVOR

Wine is complicated, with endless variations to consider, from vintage years to quality tiers. However, experts know that a few basic variables shape wine's flavor, and they use those variables to make useful generalizations. For the novice, however, it's easy to miss the forest for the trees and get bogged down in overly specific details. It is far more helpful to step back, look at the big picture, and focus on the controlling factors that shape all wines, rather than the nuances that set each wine apart.

WINE'S THREE FLAVOR FACTORS
LOOKING BEYOND WINE'S MAIN INGREDIENT

Grape varieties are prominent on wine labels— they seem to offer a clear-cut way to anticipate how a wine will taste in the same way that flavor labels on ice creams do. However, grape variety is just one of three variables that control any given wine's flavor and style. The vineyard environment, meaning its terrain, soil, topography, and climate conditions, will play just as strong a role, as will the actions taken by the vintner in the process of growing the fruit and making the wine.

"The magic of the wine grape is its incredible capacity to express the diversity of nature: a single grape varietal can create wines as different as the sun and the moon." *JeB*

FACTORS IN FLAVOR AND STYLE

1

THE FRUIT FACTOR
THE GRAPE VARIETY

2

THE VINEYARD FACTOR
THE LAND'S GEOGRAPHY, CLIMATE, AND TERRAIN

3

THE HUMAN FACTOR
THE VINTNER'S GRAPE-GROWING AND WINEMAKING CHOICES

THE GRAPE

Each grape variety used for winemaking has its own unique characteristics and flavor profile. Some grapes taste quite unique, while others are less distinctive. Since wines are made of 100% grapes, the variety used will have a significant effect on how a wine will taste . . . but still, it can be trumped by other variables. Unlike ice creams—where vanilla and chocolate flavors taste fairly consistent no matter who makes them—wines from Chardonnay or Pinot Noir grapes can taste wildly different depending on where and how they were made. Grape varieties are addressed in greater depth in Chapter 5.

THE LAND

In flavor terms, wine is more deeply affected by where it is grown than most agricultural products are. Every aspect of the vineyard's geography, from its microclimates to its terrain, will be expressed in how its wine will taste. Ask any winemaker, and they will tell you that the vineyard has a greater impact on how a wine will taste than the grape variety that was planted or anything that takes place at the winery. Every factor that affects the vine and its grapes will eventually be reflected and amplified in the glass.

THE VINTNER

Much of wine's flavor is determined by its grape variety and its vineyard. However, human decisions as to how the fruit is cultivated and how the wine is made also significantly impact how a wine will taste. From which grapes to plant where to when to harvest for optimum results, farming choices made in the vineyard have a direct effect on a given wine's flavor profile. The question of how to manage the life cycle of the land—by either conventional, organic, or Biodynamic farming—also is critical in determining the potential for quality and flavor complexity.

Winemaking decisions at the winery play a major role in a wine's flavor as well. Like a chef given fresh ingredients, the winemaker chooses what to do with them: whether to make sweet wine or dry, red wine or white, wine that is fresh and unoaked or wine that is barrel-aged and refined. By manipulating the winemaking process, the winemaker can also turn the grapes into sparkling wine with bubbles or fortified wine with extra alcohol.

TASTE THE SUNSHINE
NAVIGATING THE WINE WORLD BY GRAPE RIPENESS

There is no single idea as powerful as ripeness for explaining how the wine world works and for predicting how different wines will taste. Any given wine's color, flavor, and alcohol content are almost direct reflections of the color, flavor, and sugar content of its grapes. However, these grape characteristics can vary dramatically based on how ripe the fruit is at the moment of harvest. Ripeness is driven by the vine's exposure to sunshine and warmth. As a result, ripeness is lower in cooler climates, like those found in France, or when grapes are picked earlier in the growing season, while ripeness is generally higher in warmer zones, like California, or when grapes are allowed to hang longer on the vine.

This concept is incredibly powerful for decoding how wines will taste, and it's also connected to all three of wine's flavor factors. Every grape variety has its own range of potential flavors and textures that depend on the fruit's degree of ripeness at harvest, from milder to bolder and from lighter to heavier. Geography and climate have a direct impact on the ripening process, narrowing a grape's possible flavor range in any given wine region or vineyard. Finally, human choices made in cultivating grapes can speed or slow ripening as well, and the winemaker's decision of precisely when to pick the fruit locks in its key flavor traits, thereby controlling how the wine will taste after the winemaking process is complete.

> " Sunshine has a more dramatic impact on grape ripeness than any other factor; it is the key to defining a wine's style." *JeB*

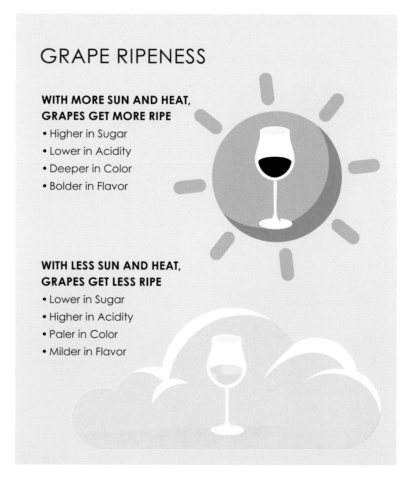

GRAPE RIPENESS

WITH MORE SUN AND HEAT, GRAPES GET MORE RIPE
• Higher in Sugar
• Lower in Acidity
• Deeper in Color
• Bolder in Flavor

WITH LESS SUN AND HEAT, GRAPES GET LESS RIPE
• Lower in Sugar
• Higher in Acidity
• Paler in Color
• Milder in Flavor

FLAVOR-MAPPING WINES

The flavor map below illustrates how wines made with the same grape can taste quite different in predictable ways. Charting wines according to their two most important power scales—tactile weight and flavor intensity—reveals how wines made with the same grape grow heavier in texture and bolder in flavor when they are grown in warmer and sunnier places. Cultural differences play a role here as well, since winemaking traditions affect the decisions vintners make in growing grapes and making wine. For example, centuries of heritage lead French vintners to embrace traditional priorities and to make lighter, drier wines designed to age gracefully and to flatter local cuisine. California has been known for a spirit of innovation, embracing science and technology in winemaking, and a warmer, sunnier climate that results in stronger, fruitier wines that please on first sip and are as often enjoyed alone as paired with food.

PATTERN RECOGNITION

Plotting wine's two most important power scales—weight and flavor intensity—on a classic grid can provide any wine drinker with expert-level insights into how wine styles relate to one another on a sensory level. Why weight and flavor? Both are key sensory characteristics that are highly relevant to personal tastes and easy to identify, though neither can sum up a wine's complexity or quality.

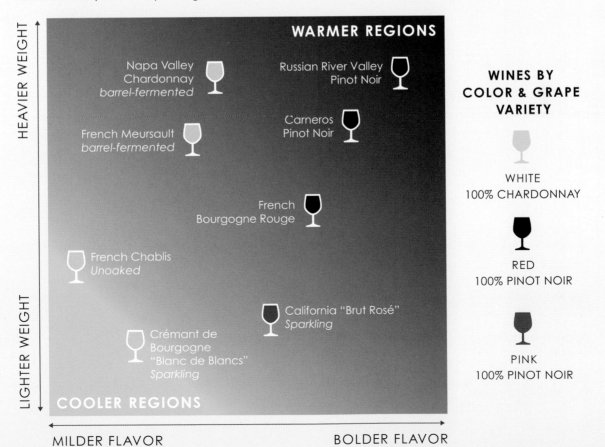

THE RIPENING PROCESS
A UNIVERSAL TRANSITION THAT SHAPES HOW WINES TASTE

Ripeness is the final stage of fruit development, when the fruit becomes ready to pick and eat. Plants get their energy from sunlight, so the degree of ripeness will always depend on how much sun the plant gets in the final weeks before harvest. Ripening shifts fruit from being hard and sour toward a softer, sweeter, and juicier state, a process that is accompanied by a color change from green to the fruit's proper color. We use the word "green" to describe how underripe fruit tastes—sour and bitter, with the leafy flavor of green vegetables—even when we talk about fruits like Granny Smith apples that remain green in color when they are fully ripe.

Winemakers must harvest their grapes at just the right moment in order to lock in the desired ratios of sugar, acids, and flavor compounds. Sugar content is the main consideration in deciding when to harvest since the amount of sugar determines wine's potential alcoholic strength, but many other components are also carefully tracked. The climate, weather, and terrain will establish the range

> "Ripeness is the most powerful indication of a wine's ultimate potential and for predicting how different wines will taste." *JeB*

of ripeness possible in any given vineyard. When winemakers want to emphasize refreshment, as with most white and rosé wines and all sparkling wines, it's common to harvest earlier at lower ripeness to preserve acidity. When they want to make stronger or bolder wines, like robust reds, winemakers often wait longer before picking so the grapes can develop extra color and flavor as they ripen.

SLIDING SCALES OF RIPENESS

Grapes become sweeter as they ripen, and their acidity also drops. Skin colors deepen, and the fruit's flavors get bolder, moving away from subtle, earthy, and leafy flavors toward the jammier, spicier flavors of baked fruit desserts.

ACIDITY

GREEN FLAVOR

SWEETNESS

SKIN COLOR

FRUIT FLAVOR

RIPENESS IS A MOVING TARGET

Just as tomatoes can be eaten when green, when fully ripe, or when shriveled and sun-dried, grapes can be suitable for winemaking at many different points on the ripeness continuum. As a result, there is no single definition of "the perfect ripeness" used to decide when to pick grapes. Not only does each fruit component respond a little differently to changes in terrain, weather, and farming methods, but the degree of desired ripeness varies widely depending on the style of wine being made.

Grapes with as little as 18% sugar would be considered fully ripe for French grapes intended to be made into a sparkling rosé in a region like Burgundy. For red wine grapes in California, though, anything below 24% sugar would be seen as unacceptably "green" and underripe. Luckily, wine drinkers need not adopt the winemaker's nuanced view of ripeness. For the purpose of navigating wine by style, it's more useful to generalize—think of the grapes used for lighter wine styles, like sparkling wines and rosés, as being "less ripe" and those used for heavier styles, like Cabernet Sauvignon or Port, as being "more ripe."

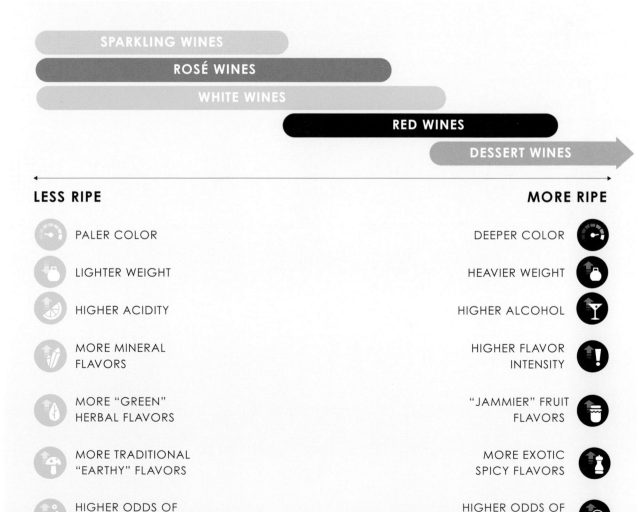

CRACKING THE WINE CODE
ALCOHOL & WINE'S SPECTRUM OF STYLE

Grapes that receive more sun become riper, which increases the overall sensory "impact" of their wine on multiple levels. Not only do riper grapes develop a higher concentration of flavor compounds, they also get sweeter. Sweeter grapes produce wines with higher alcohol when they are fermented all the way to dryness. The most noticeable effect of greater alcoholic strength is to make wines feel noticeably richer in texture, but alcohol has another, more subliminal effect that's as important to winemakers as it is to perfumers: it evaporates easily and in doing so amplifies scent and flavor.

Even half a degree of extra alcohol can make wine seem stronger and more concentrated in flavor, so both factors add up to make wines made from riper grapes taste considerably bolder. Being riper leads grapes to taste stronger even before they're fermented into wine, but once that happens, they taste doubly intense thanks to the scent-boosting properties of alcohol. So what does this mean? It means that knowing where a wine falls on the ripeness spectrum does not simply tell us whether it will feel lighter or heavier on the palate, but also whether it's likely to taste milder and more subtle or bolder and more intense.

MORE SUN

MORE SUGAR

MORE FLAVOR IMPACT

MORE   ALCOHOL

LESS SUN

LESS SUGAR

LESS FLAVOR IMPACT

LESS   ALCOHOL

> It's often possible to guess a wine's degree of ripeness from its alcohol content alone, an essential step in making sense of the confusing world of wine." *JeB*

WINE BY NUMBERS

In dry wines (where no grape sweetness is preserved), there is a nearly direct relationship between ripeness and alcohol content. Since alcohol content must be listed on virtually all wine labels, we can predict a fair amount about how a given wine will taste just by knowing that 13.5% to 14% is the norm. Wines with higher alcohol will, by definition, feel heavier than average, but we can also guess that they will taste more intense and less tart due to greater ripeness. Dry wines, with lower alcohol, will usually be the reverse: lighter, milder, and more acidic.

For those willing to make some generalizations, the predictive power of alcohol content doesn't stop there. Some wine factors that are entirely under human control, such as degrees of oak and carbonation, are associated with higher or lower degrees of ripeness (and therefore alcohol content) for purely aesthetic reasons. The likelihood that a wine will be oaky increases greatly with higher alcohol levels, for example, while a lower-than-average alcohol level increases the chances of encountering carbonation. There are exceptions to these rules of thumb, of course, and wine qualities are the least foreseeable in the crowded middle ground, but these patterns hold true enough to provide useful guidance for beginners. It's also helpful to know that the further a wine's alcohol levels deviate from the norm, the more accurate these rules are.

READ THE FINE PRINT

One of the most useful pieces of information on any wine label is hidden in the small print, whether on the front or back label: the percentage of alcohol it contains. A wine's alcohol content is required to be listed on most wine labels and correlates well enough to many wine traits to serve as a rough indicator of style.

EXPECT LOW RIPENESS TRAITS	EXPECT MEDIUM RIPENESS TRAITS	EXPECT HIGH RIPENESS TRAITS
Always lighter in weight	Always midweight	Always heavier in weight
Usually higher acidity	Usually moderate acidity	Usually lower acidity
Milder flavor & paler color	Moderate flavor & color depth	Bolder flavor & deeper color
Rarely oaked; often bubbly	Often oaked; rarely bubbly	Usually oaked; never bubbly

UNDERSTANDING TERROIR
THE FLAVOR IMPRINT OF THE VINEYARD

Wine experts know that the region of origin has the most significant impact on how wines taste and is the main factor that gives wines their individuality. Everything about a vineyard informs how its wine will taste, from macrolevel factors of geography like latitude to microlevel nuances like soil composition, and from unchangeable features like terrain to variables like the weather at harvesttime.

"The tastes of grapes and winemaking may seem more apparent, but it is the flavors of the earth that breathe life into wine's unique sense of place." *JeB*

LOCATION, LOCATION, LOCATION

Many confusing aspects of wine start to make more sense once you understand two central concepts about the importance of the land:

- **A wine's appellation, or formal region of origin, is its most important quality factor.** Exceptional wines can only come from great vineyard sites. Pinot Noir may be a noble grape, but it needs very specific growing conditions to perform well: its wine wouldn't taste good if it was grown in Siberia or in the Sahara. Appellations are formal regions of wine origin that signal the value of a vineyard's real estate in terms of the quality potential of its wines. Just as oranges from Florida command premium prices, so do wines from famous wine-growing regions like Napa Valley or Burgundy.

- **The smallest appellations are the most prestigious and almost always make superior wine.** Specificity about where a wine's grapes were grown is an indicator of quality potential; therefore, smaller appellations command higher prices. There is no economic incentive to go to the trouble of legally recognizing a subappellation inside of a larger one unless the land has a proven track record of making finer, more distinctive wines.

As a result, the most historic wine regions that make the finest wines typically have the most complicated appellation structures. In Europe, the smallest appellations are also subject to the strictest quality standards. Burgundy's largest appellation, Bourgogne, encompasses 100 others that descend in scale from regions to districts to villages and smaller still, to the level of single-vineyard sites. The most highly-regarded are a few dozen *Grand Crus*, or single-vineyard appellations, that denote the very best Burgundy wines and are subject to extraordinarily rigorous minimum standards in their grape growing and winemaking.

THE TASTE OF THE PLACE

Terroir means "earth" or "soil" in everyday French, but the term has been adopted in the wine trade to refer to sensory traits that are location specific. Terroir is often described as an "earthy" or "mineral" flavor, but it can manifest itself in a wine's texture or finish as well. Terroir is hard for the average wine drinker to discern. If wine were music, terroir wouldn't be a melody or arrangement—it would be the distinctive acoustics of a specific performance venue, like the famed resonance of Carnegie Hall.

Reading about terroir, it's natural to wonder if there's actual dirt in your wine. There isn't, but it has been known for centuries that vineyard soil plays a strong role in wine flavor, and more recently it has become clear that farming choices can amplify or suppress wine's terroir traits. The mechanisms aren't fully understood, but the interplay of life cycles in the vine's environment appear to hold the answer, particularly microbiological activity such as soil renewal and fermentation. The systemic chemical treatments associated with conventional farming are certainly known to weaken wine's terroir. This suggests a tasteable connection to the web of life belowground that leads many premium vintners to practice organic or natural agriculture or even Biodynamic farming.

TASTEABLE ENVIRONMENT

Vineyard soils and ecosystems are major quality factors in grape growing, and their effects can be tasted in the wine glass.

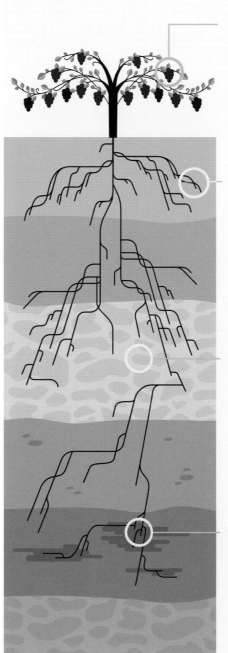

Fingerprint of Flavor
Vineyard-specific nuances of taste that might not be apparent in fresh grapes can be exposed in wine through fermentation.

Biome Belowground
From earthworms to fungi, a complex web of life sustains healthy vineyard soils and contributes to wine's distinctive terroir.

Soil Composition
Winemakers have known for centuries that soil type and composition—whether limestone or clay, heavier soils, or rocky, well-drained soils—as well as variations in mineral and nutrient content, result in consistent flavor changes in wine.

Root Depth
Vines that must dig deep for water are the most resilient, producing better fruit during both droughts and stormy seasons.

CULTIVATING QUALITY
WHY FARMING METHODS MATTER

Grapes for easy-drinking value wines are cultivated very differently from those destined for fine wines. Nowadays, people are well aware that how fruits and vegetables are grown affects how they taste— tomatoes from our own gardens taste more flavorful than factory-farmed supermarket tomatoes, for example. The same principles apply to wine grapes. Vineyards making bulk wines and vineyards making premium wines are managed with opposing priorities in terms of crop volumes and agricultural philosophies.

The growers of grapes used to make value-oriented wines must maximize efficiency. Farming for the mass market requires irrigation and chemical interventions like fertilizers and fungicides to boost crop volume and keep prices low. To reduce yields and maximize flavor, quality-minded vintners farm quite differently: often by hand and in harmony with the land. Since bumper crops dilute flavor, grape yields per vine are deliberately suppressed to increase wine's concentration. More importantly, though, ambitious vintners know that their fruit must be cultivated as naturally as possible to achieve greatness, with little or no chemical intervention in order to fully express the terroir.

MASS-MARKET WINES   Grapes per vine: 12-20 lbs • Fruit per acre: 7-10 tons • Bottles per acre: 5,000-7,500

SITE SELECTION
- Flat, tractor-friendly vineyard sites
- Fertile, water-retaining soils
- Low-cost real estate (generic regional appellation like "California")

VINEYARD MANAGEMENT
- Higher crop yields (up to 10 tons/acre)
- Conventional farming with chemical inputs
- Irrigation
- Mechanized harvesting
- Vintner purchases fruit from many vineyards and growers

LUXURY WINES   Grapes per vine: 2-7 lbs • Fruit per acre: 1.5-4 tons • Bottles per acre: 1,000-3,000

SITE SELECTION
- Steeper hillside vineyard sites
- Low-fertility, well-drained soils
- High-cost real estate (prestige district appellation like "Napa Valley")

VINEYARD MANAGEMENT
- Lower crop yields (as low as 1.5 tons/acre)
- Natural, organic or Biodynamic farming with no chemicals
- Dry-farming
- Hand harvesting
- Vintner grows their own fruit on their own land (aka "estate grown")

> Natural farming, in harmony with nature, is not simply about doing what's best for the environment. It's also about farming for quality, growing the best possible fruit to make the best possible wine." *Jeb*

ORGANIC CERTIFICATION

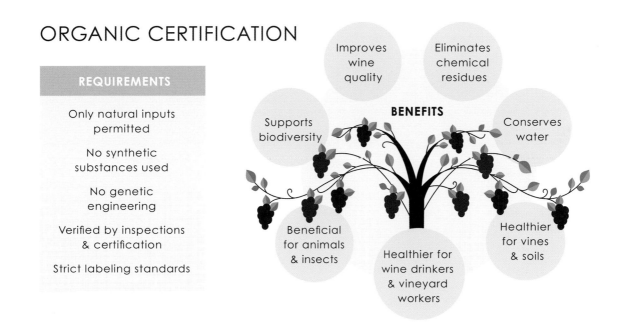

REQUIREMENTS

Only natural inputs permitted

No synthetic substances used

No genetic engineering

Verified by inspections & certification

Strict labeling standards

BENEFITS

Improves wine quality

Eliminates chemical residues

Supports biodiversity

Conserves water

Beneficial for animals & insects

Healthier for wine drinkers & vineyard workers

Healthier for vines & soils

WHAT DOES IT MEAN TO BE "ORGANIC"?

The word "organic" is a ballpark term used to describe carbon-based compounds and living matter of all kinds. "Organic farming" is something much more specific: an agricultural movement that rejects the twentieth century's embrace of synthetic agricultural chemicals and genetic engineering and that advocates a return to traditional farming techniques. Prior to the Industrial Revolution, all farming was "organic" by today's standards, but the agricultural norm now involves boosting productivity with chemicals, from fungicides to pesticides, all of which are routine for conventional grape growing, too. However, many vintners have long known that reducing or eliminating the use of chemicals in vineyards, and thereby increasing life in the soil, increases wine's quality.

Not all premium wines are made from organic grapes, but the finer the wine, the more likely it is to have been cultivated as naturally as possible to improve its taste. Some vintners go to the effort to certify their grapes as organic to convey this commitment to their customers. Grape growers who meet rigorous standards and avoid all synthetic treatments can apply to have their fruit certified as organic and use the term on their wine label.

THE BIODYNAMIC ECOSYSTEM
DRAWING INSPIRATION FROM ANCIENT PRACTICES

Many modern vintners who farm organically choose to follow an even more rigorous and sustainable standard known as "Biodynamic" viticulture. All Biodynamic culture is organic, but not all organic culture is Biodynamic. First explored by the Austrian philosopher Rudolf Steiner in the early twentieth century, Biodynamic farming embraces the principle that a vineyard lies between the cosmos above and the earth below and is heavily influenced by both. The vineyard is conceived of as a whole, single, living organism of plants and animals that can be brought into self-regulating balance with as few outside inputs as possible.

Biodynamic farming stimulates biodiversity, treating the vineyard as a self-contained ecosystem. The focus is on sustaining healthy life cycles for all organisms in the vineyard—from the grapevine to the earthworm and beyond—in order to maintain a natural equilibrium that prevents maladies and disease, rather than curing them. In that sense, Biodynamic farming is preventive health in the vineyards. It fosters a natural balance between the earth, the vine, and the people caring for the vineyard, with the goal of producing wines true to their source and expressive of their unique site or terroir.

While organic regulations prohibit treating soil, wines, or fruit with synthetic chemicals, Biodynamic principles prohibit even naturally derived treatments if they are not native to the vineyard site. For example, an organic grower could purchase imported bat guano as a fertilizer, but a Biodynamic grower would rely on their own compost and the manure of their own livestock.

In Biodynamic farming, five "actors"—the soil, the plants, the animals, the Vineyardist, and the influence of the world and cosmos beyond—must all work together to achieve the goals of sustainability and wholeness: to create a healthy, cohesive ecosystem and to craft quality wine.

> "Our role as vintners is to carefully observe and embrace the rhythms of Mother Nature in order to allow extraordinary sites to speak. We farm in synergy with her to produce wines that vibrate and transcend expectations! We are all actors in the Theater of Nature!"
>
> JeB

THE SOIL

Healthy, nutrient-rich soil is at the heart of Biodynamic farming. Vineyards are treated with preparations derived from other parts of the ecosystem (such as compost, manure, and herbal tinctures) to promote plant and soil health and fight disease.

THE PLANTS

To cultivate healthy grapevines, conserve water, and minimize the need for chemical inputs, Biodynamic farming promotes techniques like planting cover crops. Cover crops connect and integrate the elements of the soil and air that are so essential for the harmonious balance of a diverse, yet unified system.

THE ANIMALS

The self-sustaining farm endeavors to attract beneficial insects as well as the bees that are so vital for pollination. Perches for hawks can help limit vertebrate pests. Cows, sheep, goats, and chickens play important roles as sources of natural manure. At least 10% of a farm should be set aside for biodiversity.

THE VINEYARDIST

The role of the Vineyardist is to ensure that everything is in the right place and happens at the right time. Guided by the phases of the moon, the sun, and the stars, they determine when the vineyard will be planted, pruned, and harvested. In the Vineyardist's hands, every drop of water and every plant, animal, and insect serves a distinct purpose in harmony with the natural cycles of the environment.

THE COSMOS

Not all natural forces are visible. All earthbound and celestial forces, visible or not, are taken into account on the living farm. For example, Biodynamic practitioners coordinate their planting, pruning, and picking with the phases of the moon, because just as the moon's gravity controls the ebb and flow of the ocean's tides, it also influences the ebb and flow of energy in the vineyard's plants and soil.

PASSION FOR WINE   THE SOURCES OF WINE'S DIVERSITY

66

HOW GRAPES BECOME WINE
INSIDE THE FERMENTATION PROCESS

Once grapes are harvested, wine is made through a process called "fermentation," where living yeast cultures convert the fruit's sugar content into alcohol. Yeasts are single-celled fungus organisms—one of the most basic forms of life—and in nature, fermentation is an early stage of spoilage. However, mankind learned long ago how to manipulate fermentation to preserve food or make it more digestible. Different types of fermentation can turn grains into bread or beer or milk into cheese or yogurt.

During their life cycle, yeasts add new flavor compounds that weren't present in the original food's raw material by generating trace amounts of esters and aldehydes during the complex chemical reactions of fermentation. Yeasts can transform the one-dimensional taste of fresh grapes into the complex and multifaceted flavor of fine wine. Thanks to yeast, wine can taste of many things—of apples or berries, of herbs or spices, even of flowers—but it very rarely tastes overtly like grapes the way grape juice or grape jelly does.

As part of their metabolic processes, yeasts consume sugar and break it down into alcohol and carbon dioxide. Since yeasts are everywhere, fermentation begins spontaneously any time a sweet liquid is exposed to air in the right temperature range—for example, juice left out of the refrigerator will start to ferment, tasting slightly carbonated and reduced in sweetness. Wild yeasts are just as widespread in vineyards and wineries as they are in your kitchen, and these yeasts are often used to make wine, particularly in the most traditional wine regions of Europe. Nowadays, though, many modern vintners prefer to inoculate their grapes with carefully cultured yeast strains to obtain more predictable results.

Grapes are sweet, but wines usually are not. There are two reasons for this. First, making dry wine is much, much easier than making sweet wine. That's because once fermentation begins, yeasts will feed and reproduce until they have completely depleted their sugar supply, and it is rather difficult to stop this process midstream. Second, dry wines were historically more desirable because they have a longer shelf life. As a result, winemaking traditions evolved around making dry wines, so winemakers usually view sugar in grapes as potential alcohol content for their dry wines, not as potential sugar content for flavor purposes.

> "Yeast has a magical ability to enhance the flavor of whatever it ferments, whether it's grapes into wine, milk into cheese, or cocoa beans into chocolate." *Jeb*

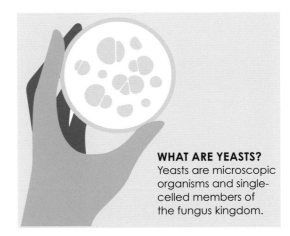

WHAT ARE YEASTS?
Yeasts are microscopic organisms and single-celled members of the fungus kingdom.

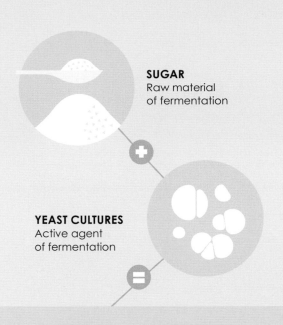

SUGAR
Raw material
of fermentation

YEAST CULTURES
Active agent
of fermentation

THE CHEMICAL EQUATION OF FERMENTATION

Alcoholic drinks begin with fermentation, where living yeasts consume and metabolize sugar, converting it into alcohol. This process also generates carbon dioxide and heat energy, as well as new flavors and aromas.

Wines are most stable when all of the sugar in the grapes has been converted to alcohol, which helps explain why most wines are fermented to complete dryness. However, it is possible to interrupt the process and sacrifice potential alcohol to preserve some grape sweetness.

MULTIPLE PRODUCTS OF FERMENTATION

ALCOHOL

CARBON DIOXIDE

NEW FLAVORS &
AROMA COMPOUNDS

HEAT ENERGY

PROGRESSION OF FERMENTATION

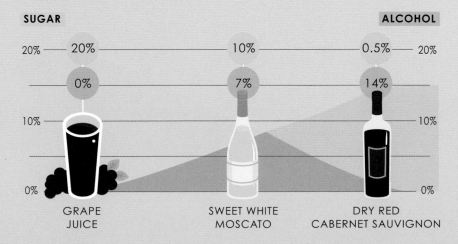

SUGAR

ALCOHOL

20%	20%	10%	0.5%	20%
0%	7%	14%
10%			10%
0%			0%

GRAPE
JUICE

SWEET WHITE
MOSCATO

DRY RED
CABERNET SAUVIGNON

WHITE WINE VS. RED WINE
DIFFERENT IN MORE THAN JUST GRAPE COLOR

The main differences between red and white wines do not derive as much from the type of grapes used as they do from the different processes by which we ferment the two styles: red wines are fermented with their skins; whites are not. As a result, reds feature the stronger flavors and slight bitterness of grape skins, while white wines have milder flavors that are derived only from the juice of the grape.

Imagine following two recipes that use the same ingredients. Peeling, straining, and chilling tomatoes with onions and peppers creates a delicate cold gazpacho soup and preserves the vegetables' garden-fresh taste. Crushing and simmering those same ingredients will produce a thicker, stronger-tasting pasta sauce. Winemakers get similar results with grapes. Making white wine involves not only removing grape skins but also fermenting the grapes in a closed vessel at colder temperatures in order to retain a fresh-picked grape flavor. Making red wine requires the opposite: maximizing grape skin contact during fermentation in open containers at warmer temperatures to extract as much of their color and flavor as possible. Since astringent tannin compounds come along for the ride in red wines but not in whites, red wines are more often aged in barrels after fermentation, a process that softens the astringency found in the peel of the grape.

> "Grapes of all colors are transparent beneath their skins. Red wines draw their color and flavor from grape skins, while whites taste purely of clear grape juice." *JeB*

TIME & TEMPERATURE

Fermentation generates heat, which must be carefully managed by winemakers. Warmth speeds the yeast life cycle, and when the yeast metabolism rate is high, new flavor compounds are generated in complex chemical reactions. These flavors and scents were not originally present in the grapes and must be carefully managed to ensure pleasant results.

Red wines are always fermented warmer and faster than whites because this helps extract color from grape skins; therefore, red wines tend to feature more yeast-generated flavors. Since vintners chill the fermenting juice when making white wines, the rate of chemical reactions that create new aromatic compounds is greatly reduced.

Hot, fast, and turbulent fermentations are needed to extract color from grape skins

1–3 WEEKS

VS

3–6 WEEKS

Cold, slow, and tranquil fermentations are needed to preserve the fresh taste of clear grape juice

WINEMAKING: WHOLE-GRAPE RED VS. JUICE-ONLY WHITE

CRUSH GRAPES

The first step for making all wines is to harvest and crush grapes. Red wines can only be made from dark-skinned grapes. White wines are usually made from green grapes but can be produced from grapes of any color.

FERMENTATION & PRESSING

The next key steps of winemaking are fermentation (where fruit sugars are converted to alcohol) and pressing (where solids like grape skins and seeds are separated from either the grape juice or the finished wine). The essential distinction between red and white wine stems from the order in which these steps take place.

RED: FERMENT WITH SOLIDS BEFORE PRESSING

Red wines must be fermented with the skins, seeds, and pulp in the tank to impart color to the clear juice. Therefore, the crushed grapes are fermented first, before the liquid wine is separated from the grape solids.

WHITE: FERMENT WITHOUT SOLIDS AFTER PRESSING

Regardless of the color of the grapes used to make a white wine, the grape juice must be separated from the crushed pulp *before* fermentation begins. Since grape juice is clear and less intensely flavored than grape skins, white wines are transparent and milder in flavor compared to red wines.

WHOLE-GRAPE RED WINEMAKING

CRUSH DARK-SKINNED GRAPES

FERMENT WHOLE GRAPES:
SKINS, SEEDS, PULP, & JUICE

PRESS TO SEPARATE WINE
FROM GRAPE SOLIDS

RED WINES
TASTE STRONGER &
MORE LIKE GRAPE PEELS

JUICE-ONLY WHITE WINEMAKING

CRUSH GRAPES OF
ANY COLOR

PRESS TO SEPARATE JUICE
FROM GRAPE SOLIDS

FERMENT GRAPE
JUICE ONLY

WHITE WINES
TASTE MILDER &
MORE LIKE GRAPE JUICE

ROSÉ WINE
WINES WITH ONLY A HINT OF COLOR

Once we know that grape pulp and juice is colorless and that red wines must therefore stew with purple grape skins to acquire their color and flavor, it becomes much easier to grasp how pink wines fit into the picture. While it is possible to make pale rosé wines from pale purple grapes like Pinot Grigio, this is almost never done in practice. Virtually all pink wines are made from the same dark-skinned grapes used for making red wines—winemakers simply shorten the period of time that the clear juice spends in contact with the dark skins in order to extract less color. Pink wines tend to fall into one of two styles—either dry or lightly sweet—depending on which of two French regions provides their inspiration:

- Most dry rosés are modeled on the pink wines of Provence and the Rhône Valley in the south of France. Here the warm, sunny climate favors red grapes over white grapes . . . but also leads locals to crave chillable wines that are more refreshing than robust reds and more flattering to their cuisine, which often features fresh produce and seafood.

- Most lightly sweet rosés are modeled on the pink wines of the chilly northern Anjou region of the Loire Valley, where red grapes can barely ripen and can taste more pleasant when harvested early and made into an off-dry "blush" wine.

> " The French word for the color pink takes its name from a beautiful flower. The rose symbolizes love, passion, and new beginnings." *JeB*

ENJOY WITHIN MONTHS OF RELEASE

By its nature, pink winemaking is a hybrid process that combines aspects of both red and white winemaking practices to produce a wine that falls between the red and white color extremes. As a result, rosé wines will always have less natural resistance to oxidation than either a standard white or red wine has, making rosés among the most fragile of all wines. Pink wines do not age gracefully—most should be consumed within months of release. They are delicious in the bloom of youth but rarely have what it takes to grow more interesting with age.

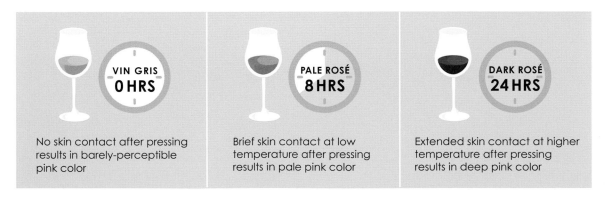

VIN GRIS 0 HRS
No skin contact after pressing results in barely-perceptible pink color

PALE ROSÉ 8 HRS
Brief skin contact at low temperature after pressing results in pale pink color

DARK ROSÉ 24 HRS
Extended skin contact at higher temperature after pressing results in deep pink color

PINK WINEMAKING

The majority of rosé wines are made in a way that combines elements of both red and white winemaking, with a carefully choreographed period of "skin contact" that determines their degree of color and flavor intensity.

This process begins the same way it does for a red wine: dark-skinned grapes are crushed. As the resulting "must" begins to ferment, color and flavor compounds from the dark grape skins are slowly extracted into the clear juice. The duration and temperature of this phase are the variables that will determine the depth and shade of the wine's pink color. A few hours spent in a chilled tank produces a faint rosy blush, while a couple of days at room temperature provides a darker fuchsia hue.

While a red wine would stew with its skins for weeks and finish its fermentation before being pressed, rosé wines must be separated from their grape solids quickly. Once the juice has acquired the right degree of color and flavor, the pink liquid is separated from the dark skins and moved to a temperature-controlled tank. From this point on, the fermentation process proceeds as it does for white wines: long, slow, and cold to preserve the freshness of the grape's flavor.

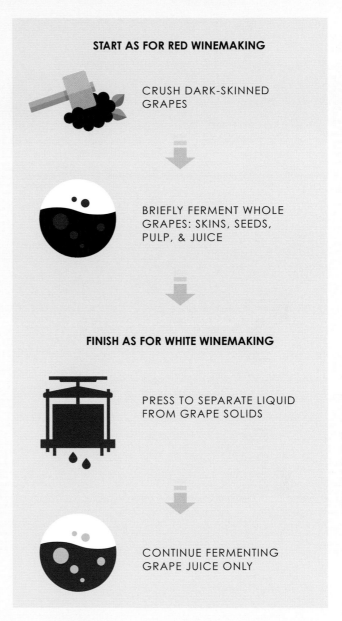

START AS FOR RED WINEMAKING

CRUSH DARK-SKINNED GRAPES

BRIEFLY FERMENT WHOLE GRAPES: SKINS, SEEDS, PULP, & JUICE

FINISH AS FOR WHITE WINEMAKING

PRESS TO SEPARATE LIQUID FROM GRAPE SOLIDS

CONTINUE FERMENTING GRAPE JUICE ONLY

EXCEPTIONS TO THE ROSÉ RULE

VIN GRIS: In this rare rosé style, whose name means "grey wine," the grape juice was historically pressed immediately, as would be done for making white wine. This imparts only a barely perceptible blush of color to the wine, which can look more faintly brassy-gold than true pink, and only a faint hint of berry flavor. However, since these words are not regulated, many standard *rosé* wines are labeled as *vin gris* purely for the marketing appeal of this French term.

BLENDED ROSÉ: Very few pink wines are made by simply blending white and red wines, but this practice is most common in sparkling wines. Since the processes that add bubbles can strip color from wine, it is more practical to simply add a splash of red wine as a final color adjustment, as pioneered in the French region of Champagne.

THE ROLE OF OAK BARRELS
REFINING WINE THROUGH MATURATION

Like all food products, wine changes over time. Unlike most foods, thanks to an uncommon balance between perishable and preservative components, wine has the potential to resist deterioration and to improve after spending months or years aging in barrels or bottles. Wines were once made and sold in barrels, but nowadays, the vast majority are fermented in inert stainless-steel tanks and sold in bottles. However, winemakers still use traditional oak barrels to refine and improve most premium wines.

> " In the same way that chefs use butter and spices to enrich and season recipes, vintners mature wine in oak barrels to add texture and flavor." *Jeb*

OAK BARRELS CHANGE WINE IN THREE WAYS

1 ALL BARRELS SOFTEN AND ENRICH WINE'S TEXTURE

Air enters through wood's pores, exposing the wine to very slow, continuous oxidation. This causes small-scale chemical reactions that soften harsh young wines and help them feel smoother on the palate.

2 ALL BARRELS INTENSIFY WINE

Water and alcohol are absorbed through wood's pores and evaporate when they reach the surface. The remaining flavor compounds, acids, and tannins become more concentrated as a result, increasing the quality and aging potential of the wine.

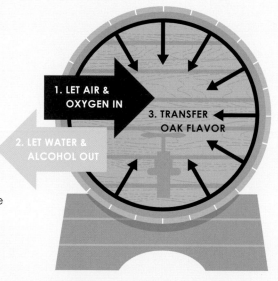

**3 ONLY NEW BARRELS ADD OAK FLAVOR
AND TANNINS TO WINE**

Oak contains soluble flavor compounds and tannins, which are imparted to wine over time. New barrels give wine a strong toasty flavor, like that found in Cognac or Bourbon. However, just as tea bags make weaker tea with each repeated use, new barrel flavors and tannins fade, too, approaching a neutral state by their fourth year. For most wines, using 100% new oak is overwhelming, so vintners typically rotate in 20%–50% new barrels when making each vintage.

DESSERT-LIKE OAK FLAVORS

Winemakers use the flavors of new oak barrels as a seasoning for wine. New oak is high in aromatic compounds that are associated with desserts, most notably vanillin. For vintners, French and American oak are as distinct as arabica and robusta beans are for coffee lovers. The degree of "toast" applied has a similar effect to the type of roast those coffee beans might receive. Smaller barrels also guarantee a stronger oak flavor in wine for the same reason that a fine espresso grind increases the intensity of coffee: more surface contact between wine and oak means more flavor is transferred.

NEW OAK BARRELS IMPART ALL OAK EFFECTS

Premium red wines are usually fermented in steel tanks, then matured in oak barrels for anywhere from 3 months to 3 years before being bottled (depending on the wine's style and ambition). Only the heaviest white wines see oak at all and are rarely aged in barrels longer than 12 months since they oxidize more quickly. Those that are "oaked" are usually barrel-fermented as well as barrel-aged, as with fine Chardonnays. For both red and white wines, newer barrels impart the strongest oak flavors, which fade with extended use. After having been used for 5 or more years, barrels become "neutral," meaning that although they will still soften and enrich wine texture, they will no longer transfer an oaky taste to the wine.

NEW OAK BARRELS
- Add oak flavor
- Enrich texture & concentrate wine

OLDER "NEUTRAL" OAK BARRELS
- Add no oak flavor
- Enrich texture & concentrate wine

ALTERNATIVE OAK TREATMENTS IMPART OAK FLAVOR ONLY

Many people enjoy whiskey-like oakiness in their wine, but creating it the traditional way is time-consuming and expensive. Nowadays, winemakers can add an oaky taste with wood chips, planks, or even oak extracts. However, none of these can replicate the other effects of aging wine in breathable barrels—namely, enrichment and concentration—so these methods are rarely used for anything but bargain wines.

"ALTERNATIVE" OAK TREATMENTS
- Add oak flavor
- Do not enrich or concentrate wine

INERT STAINLESS-STEEL TANKS IMPART NO OAK EFFECTS

Wines that are "unoaked" are fermented in vessels that impart no flavor, typically in temperature-controlled stainless-steel tanks for a few months before they are bottled and sold. Most white and rosé wines are unoaked, but only the lightest, youngest, and least ambitious red wines are made this way.

STAINLESS-STEEL TANKS
- Add no oak flavor
- Do not enrich or concentrate wine
- Preserve fresh taste

SPARKLING WINE
WINES WITH BUBBLES

All wines are bubbly at some point—carbon dioxide is a byproduct of fermenting sugar into alcohol. However, this natural carbonation is usually allowed to dissipate. Why? Because it is much easier to allow carbon dioxide to escape than it is to keep wine under pressure to preserve carbonation. Besides, unlike beers, wines do not need bubbles to taste refreshing, thanks to the bracingly high acidity found in grapes.

While wines that "sparkled" existed prior to the Industrial Revolution, it was not possible to capture and preserve significant carbonation until sufficiently strong bottles could be manufactured. "Sparkling wine" as we know it was an innovation

" Sparkling wines have a unique talent for stimulating our senses—they capture in a bottle the passion of a moment in time, with all its treasures and promises." *JeB*

of the nineteenth century, pioneered in the Champagne region of France. Today, virtually all fine sparkling wine is made by what we now call the "Champagne method." Lesser sparkling wines, like Prosecco and Moscato, are made by other methods that are faster and simpler and therefore less expensive.

	CHAMPAGNE METHOD	PROSECCO METHOD	ASTI METHOD
TECHNIQUE	Fermented twice; second time in sealed bottles	Fermented twice; second time in pressurized tanks	Fermented only once; in pressurized tanks
KEY FLAVOR FACTOR	Flavor and texture are enriched by long-term aging on lees (sediments)	Bottled young with no aging (to preserve fresh fruit flavors)	To preserve sweetness, fermentation is stopped halfway to completion
CARBONATION	Fine, small bubbles; long-lasting creamy mousse	Medium bubbles; persistent foamy mousse	Larger, coarser bubbles; short-lived frothy mousse
SWEETNESS	Most often very dry to medium-dry	Most often medium-dry to lightly sweet	Always fully sweet

TERMS OF SWEETNESS
Sparkling wine labels often designate their degree of sweetness with a special set of terms. The finest sparkling wines tend to fall in the "Brut" category, meaning that they have no perceptible sweetness on the palate.

Less than 6g/L Sugar

EXTRA BRUT

Less than 9g/L Sugar

BRUT

Less than 15g/L Sugar

EXTRA DRY

CRÉMANT & THE CHAMPAGNE METHOD

The rigorous Champagne method, also known as the "traditional method," is used for all of the world's best sparkling wines because of the unrivaled quality of its results. French wines made by this method outside the Champagne region are labeled "Crémant" and named for their origin, as in "Crémant de Bourgogne" from Burgundy.

STEP 1
MAKE A BASE WINE
Grapes are picked underripe and made into a lightweight dry white wine, typically from a mix of red and white grapes.

STEP 2
ADD SUGAR & YEAST
Live yeast cultures are added along with measured doses of cane sugar and sealed in individual bottles. Aged base wines from previous vintages may also be added to deepen flavor.

STEP 4
AGING ON THE LEES
Once sugar is depleted, yeasts die and form a sludgy sediment known as "lees." Time spent in contact with the lees (in French, *sur lies*) enriches texture and adds a desirable flavor of baked goods. All Champagne and Crémant must age at least 18 months sur lies, but some may age up to 10 years.

STEP 3
SECOND FERMENTATION
Yeasts consume sugar and convert it into alcohol and carbon dioxide.

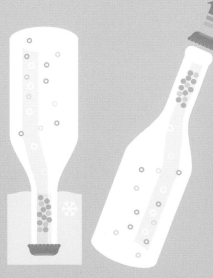

STEP 5
SEDIMENT REMOVAL
A process called "riddling" is used to slowly invert bottles. Once the lees rest on the cap, the bottle neck is submerged in a freezing brine solution to trap the sediment in frozen wine. When the bottle is opened, this ice plug is forced out.

STEP 6
FINAL SWEETENING
Bottles must be replenished with wine before they are corked. Red wine is used if a rosé style is desired. Since 2nd fermentations leave wine tasting extremely dry, a tiny measured amount of sugar, known as the *dosage*, is also added at this stage.

UNDERSTANDING WINE QUALITY
FOUR ELEMENTS THAT MOST FINE WINES SHARE

While there are many points of distinction between fines wines and their everyday brethren, these four elements are of such importance that they help the uninitiated make sense of wine.

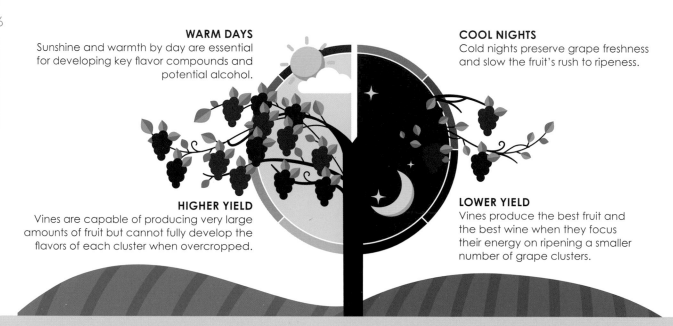

WARM DAYS
Sunshine and warmth by day are essential for developing key flavor compounds and potential alcohol.

COOL NIGHTS
Cold nights preserve grape freshness and slow the fruit's rush to ripeness.

HIGHER YIELD
Vines are capable of producing very large amounts of fruit but cannot fully develop the flavors of each cluster when overcropped.

LOWER YIELD
Vines produce the best fruit and the best wine when they focus their energy on ripening a smaller number of grape clusters.

CLIMATE—SUNNY DAYS, COOL NIGHTS

The world's finest wines are made in regions where there is a big swing in temperature, from the daytime high to the nighttime low, during the final weeks of the grape-growing season. Fruit develops its best possible flavors when it gets ample sunshine and warmth by day to boost its ripening process and then cool nights to slow its rush to ripeness. Sun is essential for making great wine, of course, but hot nights can result in wines that taste more like cooked fruit than fresh fruit. Whether they are caused by ocean breezes or clear desert skies, cold nights act almost like a refrigerator—low temperatures preserve freshness by postponing the drop in grape acidity and retaining the desirable herbal and mineral flavors associated with early stages of ripeness.

VINEYARD—LOW FRUIT YIELDS PER VINE

Quantity and quality rarely go hand in hand, and wine is no exception. Producers of value wines must aim for bumper crops to keep their prices competitive, which usually requires irrigation and chemical fertilizers to boost fruit tonnage per acre. Top-notch vintners, however, rigorously prune vines back to lower yields per vine, and they irrigate sparingly—if at all—to prevent dilution. Limiting the number of clusters of grapes per plant results in higher levels of critical sugars, acids, and flavor compounds, all of which boost wine's concentration and quality potential. Some vintners even trim off immature fruit in a "green harvest" before the final ripening stage in order to focus the energy of each plant on making the most of the remaining grapes.

> "Better wine is produced today than at any point in human history now that we know how to nurture greatness from the vineyard all the way to the glass." *Jeb*

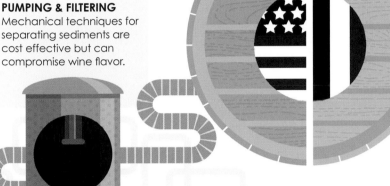

AMERICAN OAK
More forceful flavors and lower costs lead American barrels to be most appropriate for shorter aging periods and more affordable wines.

PUMPING & FILTERING
Mechanical techniques for separating sediments are cost effective but can compromise wine flavor.

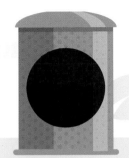

GRAVITY FLOW & FINING
Gentle methods of separating sediments are used to preserve flavor and complexity in fine wines.

FRENCH OAK
More subtle and more expensive, French barrels are prized by winemakers for the longer aging required by premium wines.

WINEMAKING—MINIMAL INTERVENTION

Whether a vintner is making white wine, red wine, or sparkling wine, one simple concept remains central to fine winemaking: gentle handling at every stage will improve how the wine tastes. While everyday wines are routinely pumped and filtered rather harshly, ambitious winemakers take greater care with smaller batches of fine wines, from hand-harvesting in the fields to hand-sorting the fruit before the crush. So-called "gravity-flow" wineries use the natural pull of the earth to move wine from one stage of winemaking to the next, without the need for hydraulic pumps. Slow and gentle "fining" of the wine allows for the removal of sediments without resorting to industrial filtration methods, which can flatten nuances of flavor along with removing unwanted solids.

AGING—FINE FRENCH OAK BARRELS

The best wines are often aged for years before they are ready to be released for sale, and most will continue to age gracefully for years if stored well. For almost all red wines and many of the richest white wines, a key phase of maturation takes place in oak barrels, which concentrate the wine and enrich its texture. White oak has proven to be the best wood for wine barrels, and the cooperage techniques pioneered in France have the longest track record of quality. As a result, winemakers around the world see fine French oak barrels as an essential ingredient in their fine wine recipes. While American oak barrels can taste quite bold and caramelized and provide a flavor familiarly associated with Bourbon, French oak is prized for its subtlety and the smoky spice of great Cognac.

CHAPTER 4

THE SPECTRUM OF STYLE

SORTING WINES BY HOW THEY TASTE

One of the most confusing aspects of wine is that two wines made from the same grape can taste completely different. Just as paintings can be loosely classified from realistic to abstract stylistically, regardless of their subject or color scheme, wines also tend to fall into a recognizable style spectrum. The key factor is grape ripeness. A little insight into the impacts of geography and climate (as well as culture and winemaking priorities) can help any beginner navigate the wine world with confidence.

THE SPECTRUM OF WINE STYLE
FLAVOR FAMILIES SHAPED BY SUNSHINE & RIPENESS

We get our energy from food; plants get theirs from sunlight. The more sun a vine gets, the riper its grapes will become, meaning that exposure to sunshine has a more direct impact on how wines taste than grape varieties or regions or barrels do. That's because the sun controls all of the flavor changes that take place during the ripening process.

More sunlight and warmth in the vineyard results in sweeter grapes that have a deeper color and more dessert-like fruit flavors, traits that are associated with stronger, darker wines. Less sunlight and warmth in the growing season have the opposite effect: the development of sugars, color, and fruity flavor compounds are suppressed, while grape acidity and the herbal, mineral flavors associated with less-ripe fruits are preserved. These traits are prized in lighter wines.

The reliability of this universal principle allows us to use it as a navigation tool for finding the wines we're most likely to love and to sort wines into broad "style categories" by how they taste and smell and feel in the mouth. While wine labels focus on regional appellations and grapes—factors that require advanced wine knowledge to interpret—the Spectrum of Style is a more user-friendly system that helpfully groups wines into five flavor families. Regardless of where they're made or from which grape, the wines in each group share similar traits, from levels of sweetness and acidity to degrees of color and flavor intensity. The Spectrum of Style flavor families ascend in weight and concentration, moving from lighter whites to deeper, heavier reds.

> "Since the key facets of wine are all driven by sunlight, we can group wines based on how they taste and how they make us feel." *JeB*

SPECTRUM OF *style*

This intuitive color-coded wine navigation system aims to share sommelier-level insights with non-professionals at a glance. Label statements like grape and region of origin are not simply cumbersome to learn, but even for those who've done copious homework, neither are adequate for predicting how a wine will taste. The Spectrum of Style looks beyond such label statements to sort Boisset Collection wines into more relevant flavor families, reflecting the direct links between grape ripeness and wine's key sensory traits, like weight, acidity, and the presence of new oak.

WHITE WINES

White wines, including rosé and sparkling wines, are divided into two flavor families:

VIVACIOUS wines may be sparkling, white, or rosé, but they are always lighter and brighter—they're tangy, refreshing wines.

VOLUPTUOUS wines are heavier whites that are richer in texture. Most are dry and oak barrel-fermented, but some are lusciously sweet dessert wines.

RED WINES

Red wines are sorted into three flavor families:

ELEGANT wines are midweight traditional reds made in the bone-dry, earthy style of food-oriented, classic French wines.

SENSUOUS wines are modern, midweight red wines that are fruitier, less tart and less tannic—truly hedonistic wines of pure pleasure.

POWERFUL wines are the boldest of the bunch: inky, age-worthy wines that are heavier and more concentrated in flavor.

VIVACIOUS WHITES & ROSÉS
BRISK WINES OF REFRESHMENT

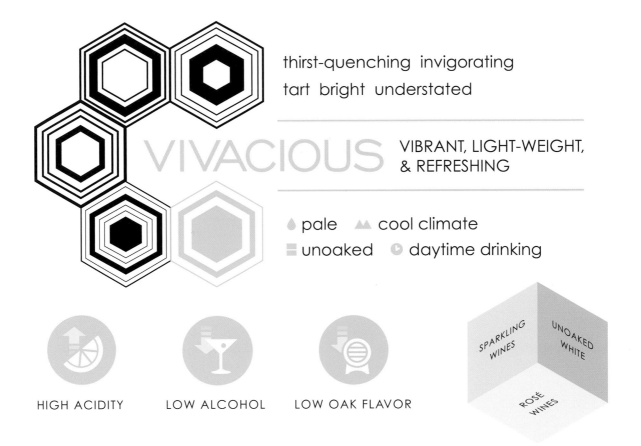

thirst-quenching invigorating
tart bright understated

VIVACIOUS

VIBRANT, LIGHT-WEIGHT,
& REFRESHING

⬦ pale   ▲▲ cool climate
▬ unoaked   ◖ daytime drinking

HIGH ACIDITY   LOW ALCOHOL   LOW OAK FLAVOR

SPARKLING WINES   UNOAKED WHITE   ROSÉ WINES

WHAT DISTINGUISHES VIVACIOUS WINES?

The Refreshment Factor—Vivacious wines feature high levels of acidity and modest levels of alcohol, a combination that cleanses the palate and makes you say "ahh." They are ideal for serving well-chilled in hot weather or for daytime drinking before the sun goes down.

Low Grape Ripeness—Vivacious wines are made from grapes that are either grown in cooler vineyards or picked earlier in the season than usual. As a result of their modest degree of ripeness, they feature lower alcohol levels, milder flavors, and higher acidity than average. These traits are ideal for wines designed to refresh the senses.

Food-Flattering Superpowers—Vivacious styles make terrific apéritifs, of course, but they are also perfect partners for lighter fare—from sushi to salads. They're ideal for dishes that are salty, tangy, spicy, vegetarian, or served cold. However, they are surprisingly adaptable to heavier foods, providing a quenching counterpoint to bolder seasonings and richer recipes. Sommeliers have long known that lighter, brighter wines with high acidity have the most versatility at the table—they taste great with almost everything, including foods that clash with most other wines.

"Vivacious is a diverse and resplendent style that includes all of our sparkling and rosé wines, as well as those whites that are lighter, brighter, and (usually) unoaked." *JeB*

VIVACIOUS WHITES & ROSÉS
IDEAL APÉRITIFS & VERSATILE FOOD PARTNERS

Cool climates and early harvesting are ideal for making these lighter wines, which show off their low degree of ripeness in flavors of fresh, tangy fruits and minerality.

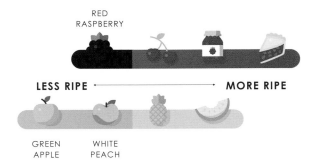

> "Lighthearted, vibrant, mischievous—Vivacious wines are inherently social. They lift the spirits, pique the appetite, and cleanse the soul." *JeB*

1   2   3   4   5

1 JCB NO. 21—BRUT
CRÉMANT DE BOURGOGNE

2 BUENA VISTA WINERY
CHAMPAGNE—LA VICTOIRE

3 J. MOREAU & FILS
CHABLIS

4 JEAN-CLAUDE BOISSET
BOURGOGNE ALIGOTÉ "LES MOUTOTS"

5 BOUCHARD AÎNÉ & FILS
POUILLY-FUISSÉ

6 JCB NO. 16
WHITE BORDEAUX BLEND

7 RAYMOND VINEYARDS
NAPA VALLEY SAUVIGNON BLANC

8 JCB NO. 5
CÔTES DE PROVENCE ROSÉ

9 DE LOACH VINEYARDS
CALIFORNIA ROSÉ

10 JCB NO. 69—BRUT
CRÉMANT DE BOURGOGNE ROSÉ

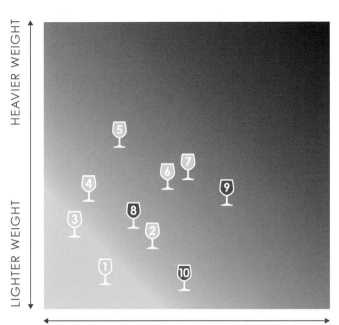

HEAVIER WEIGHT

LIGHTER WEIGHT

MILDER FLAVOR   BOLDER FLAVOR

This flavor map shows how Vivacious wines relate to one another by charting them according to two of wine's key intensity scales. Lighter to heavier weight refers to wine's texture and is loosely analogous to alcohol content in dry wines. Milder to bolder flavor refers to wine's overall flavor impact, which includes both fruit and oak flavors. Neither metric can capture the complexity and length of finish that are the hallmarks of quality in wine, of course, but they can be useful for navigating style options and for pairing wines with different foods.

6   7   8   9   10

VOLUPTUOUS WHITES
RICHLY TEXTURED WINES OF OPULENCE

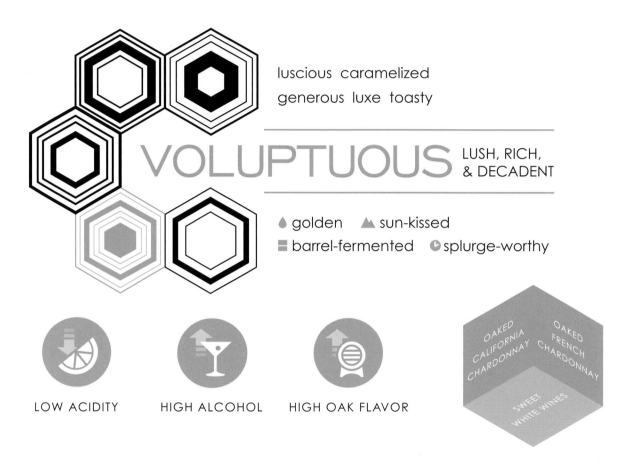

luscious caramelized
generous luxe toasty

VOLUPTUOUS LUSH, RICH, & DECADENT

◆ golden   ▲ sun-kissed
▬ barrel-fermented   ◔ splurge-worthy

OAKED CALIFORNIA CHARDONNAY

OAKED FRENCH CHARDONNAY

SWEET WHITE WINES

LOW ACIDITY   HIGH ALCOHOL   HIGH OAK FLAVOR

WHAT DISTINGUISHES VOLUPTUOUS WINES?

The Opulence Factor—Voluptuous wines offer a luxurious mouthfeel that envelopes the palate in creamy richness—quite a contrast to the bracing bite of Vivacious wines. They needn't be served ice-cold and are better suited to cool evenings and cooked foods than summer salads. These wines caress the palate with a decadent pleasure, much like slipping on a cashmere sweater or nuzzling a fluffy kitten.

High Grape Ripeness—Voluptuous wines are made from grapes that are either grown in warmer vine-yards or picked later than Vivacious styles are harvested. Their greater degree of ripeness results in bolder fruit flavors, higher alcohol, and lower acidity than most other whites. These traits lead wine-makers to use barrel fermentation and aging to further enrich the wine's texture and add the nutty flavors of new oak, reminiscent of those found in fine Cognac or Bourbon.

Caramelized Flavor—Oak-aging develops a toasty character that leads Voluptuous wines to taste less like fresh fruit and more like baked fruit desserts. This caramelized quality means that they pair better with cooked foods—sautéed, grilled, roasted, or toasted—than with pristine raw foods. These wines shine with recipes that feature flavor accents like butter, onions, garlic, or sesame oil.

"**Voluptuous** is a denser, richer style whose white wines are usually dry and barrel-fermented, but occasionally late-harvested and sweet." *JeB*

VOLUPTUOUS WHITES
GRACEFUL FOOD WINES & TREASURED INDULGENCES

Making these richer white wines requires warmer weather and longer hang time on the vine to achieve higher degrees of grape ripeness. This ripeness is captured in flavors of extra-juicy fruits, baked goods, and toasted nuts.

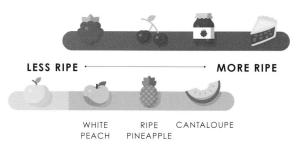

LESS RIPE ←——————→ MORE RIPE

WHITE PEACH   RIPE PINEAPPLE   CANTALOUPE

"Luscious, exquisite, alluring—Voluptuous wines offer a taste of the good life. They radiate refinement and bathe the palate in luxury." *JeB*

1   2   3   4   5

1 FORTANT
   COAST SELECT MUSCAT

2 JEAN-CLAUDE BOISSET
   BOURGOGNE CHARDONNAY

3 ROPITEAU FRÈRES
   MEURSAULT

4 BOUCHARD AÎNÉ & FILS
   CHASSAGNE-MONTRACHET
   PREMIER CRU—LES CHENEVOTTES

5 DOMAINE DE LA VOUGERAIE
   BÂTARD-MONTRACHET—GRAND CRU

6 BUENA VISTA WINERY
   CARNEROS CHARDONNAY

7 DE LOACH VINEYARDS—O.F.S.
   RUSSIAN RIVER VALLEY CHARDONNAY

8 RAYMOND VINEYARDS
   NAPA VALLEY CHARDONNAY

9 JCB NO. 33
   RUSSIAN RIVER VALLEY CHARDONNAY

10 NEIGE—PREMIÈRE
   QUÉBEC APPLE ICE WINE

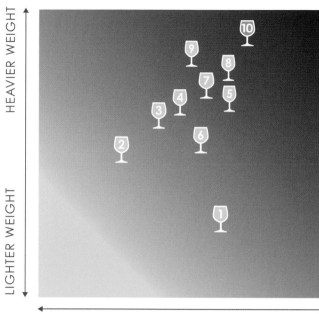

HEAVIER WEIGHT

LIGHTER WEIGHT

MILDER FLAVOR   BOLDER FLAVOR

This flavor map shows how Vivacious wines relate to one another by charting them according to two of wine's key intensity scales. Lighter to heavier weight refers to wine's texture and is loosely analogous to alcohol content in dry wines. Milder to bolder flavor refers to wine's overall flavor impact, which includes both fruit and oak flavors. Neither metric can capture the complexity and length of finish that are the hallmarks of quality in wine, of course, but they can be useful for navigating style options and for pairing wines with different foods.

6   7   8   9   10

ELEGANT REDS
UNDERSTATED WINES OF GASTRONOMY

sophisticated French-inspired
mouth-watering time-honored

ELEGANT
TRADITIONAL, EARTHY, & COMPLEX

◆ bone-dry ▬ classically styled
▲ cool climate 🕐 food-oriented

HIGH ACIDITY   HIGH EARTHY FLAVOR   LOW OAK FLAVOR

FRENCH RED BURGUNDY

REDS FROM THE SOUTH OF FRANCE

FRENCH-STYLE CALIFORNIA PINOT NOIR

WHAT DISTINGUISHES ELEGANT WINES?

The Gastronomy Factor—Elegant wines can be an acquired taste since they are not designed to seduce on the first sip but, rather, are crafted to flatter classic cuisine. They are made following methods refined over centuries in Burgundy, which include picking fruit at lower degrees of ripeness than those used to make more modern reds. They are ideal partners for European-style dishes that are driven by salt and fat but rarely perform as well with the sweeter, spicier sauces of Asia and the Americas.

Lower Grape Ripeness—Elegant wines tend to hail from cool climates, or they may be made from fruit harvested earlier in warmer zones (since high levels of grape acidity are essential for making traditional, food-oriented wines). Because of their moderate degree of ripeness, they also tend to feature lower-than-average alcohol levels and red berry flavors, all traits that lead winemakers to use a delicate hand with new oak during maturation.

Earth Tones Of Flavor—Elegant wines may not be forceful, but their depth and complexity of flavor can be truly epic—when grapes are less ripe, the rustic, earthy dimension of wine's scent becomes more dominant than its sweet, fruity flavors. Known as *terroir*, this earthiness gives Elegant wines their *je ne sais quoi*, a nuanced and savory quality that is particularly prized in fine Burgundy wines.

> "Elegant reds are lighter and leaner than most. Almost all are Pinot Noirs but only those made in the traditional earthy French style where flattering food is wine's highest purpose." JeB

ELEGANT REDS
EARTHY & ETHEREAL WINES DESIGNED FOR FOOD

Because high acidity is essential for both flattering food and graceful aging, traditional French winemaking requires fruit of lower degrees of ripeness than what more modern styles offer. This results in brighter, tangier red fruit flavors with complex, earth-toned aromatics.

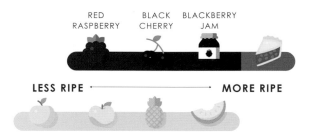

RED RASPBERRY   BLACK CHERRY   BLACKBERRY JAM

LESS RIPE ←——————→ MORE RIPE

" Restrained, graceful, seductive—Elegant wines are visceral and intimate reminders of our history. They transcend the intellect to transport us to another place and time." JeB

1   2   3   4   5

1 CHÂTEAU DE PIERREUX—BROUILLY
   LA RÉSERVE DU CHÂTEAU

2 MOMMESSIN—LA CLÉ ST. PIERRE
   BOURGOGNE PINOT NOIR

3 BOUCHARD AÎNÉ & FILS
   BEAUNE PREMIER CRU—CLOS DU ROI

4 JEAN-CLAUDE BOISSET
   GEVREY-CHAMBERTIN

5 DOMAINE DE LA VOUGERAIE
   CLOS DE VOUGEOT—GRAND CRU

6 BONPAS
   CHÂTEAUNEUF-DU-PAPE

7 JCB NO. 11
   SONOMA COAST PINOT NOIR

8 DE LOACH VINEYARDS
   RUSSIAN RIVER VALLEY PINOT NOIR

9 DE LOACH VINEYARDS
   ESTATE PINOT NOIR

10 BUENA VISTA WINERY
    THE ARISTOCRAT RED BLEND

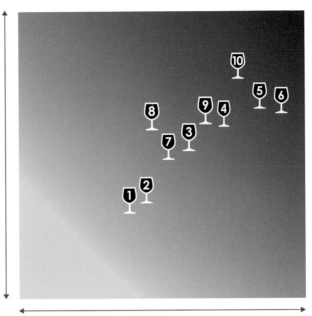

This flavor map shows how Vivacious wines relate to one another by charting them according to two of wine's key intensity scales. Lighter to heavier weight refers to wine's texture and is loosely analogous to alcohol content in dry wines. Milder to bolder flavor refers to wine's overall flavor impact, which includes both fruit and oak flavors. Neither metric can capture the complexity and length of finish that are the hallmarks of quality in wine, of course, but they can be useful for navigating style options and for pairing wines with different foods.

SENSUOUS REDS
MIDWEIGHT WINES OF PURE PLEASURE

midweight smooth modern
captivating hedonistic

SENSUOUS JUICY, SOFT, & LIP-SMACKING

● jammy ◐ immediate gratification
▬ dessert-like ▲ hyper-ripe

LOW ACIDITY   HIGH FRUIT FLAVOR   LOW TANNINS

CALIFORNIA-STYLE PINOT NOIR   FRENCH RED BEAUJOLAIS   CALIFORNIA RED BLENDS & MERLOT

WHAT DISTINGUISHES SENSUOUS WINES?

The Pure Pleasure Factor—Sensuous wines are a reflection of modern times, when many wine drinkers are more interested in a wine's wow factor upon the first sip than in traditional pursuits like cellaring wines long-term or enjoying them with specific foods. The wines in this group are unusually diverse, including everything from lighter Gamays and Pinot Noirs to denser Merlots and Cabernet blends. What makes them Sensuous is their easy-drinking style—neither as lean and green as Elegant wines nor as dense and tannic as Powerful reds.

High Grape Ripeness—Sensuous wines are made from grapes that are quite ripe, typically grapes from warmer vineyard regions. As a result of their elevated ripeness, they tend to feature lower acidity, bolder fruit flavors, and softer tannins than other red wines. These traits give Sensuous wines a juicy character and a plush, velvety mouthfeel that makes them crowd-pleasers, particularly suitable for impromptu gatherings or relaxing at home with a glass of wine after a long day.

Dessert-Like Aromatics—Advances in grape growing and winemaking have made it possible for wines to be fully dry yet smell and taste of ripe fruit or even baked fruit desserts . . . and to do so without seeming austerely acidic, tannic, or harsh. The generous core of jam-like fruit flavors in Sensuous wines tastes outstanding alone, but that core means that Sensuous wines can also pair well with foods whose levels of sugar or spice make them problematic to pair with other red wines.

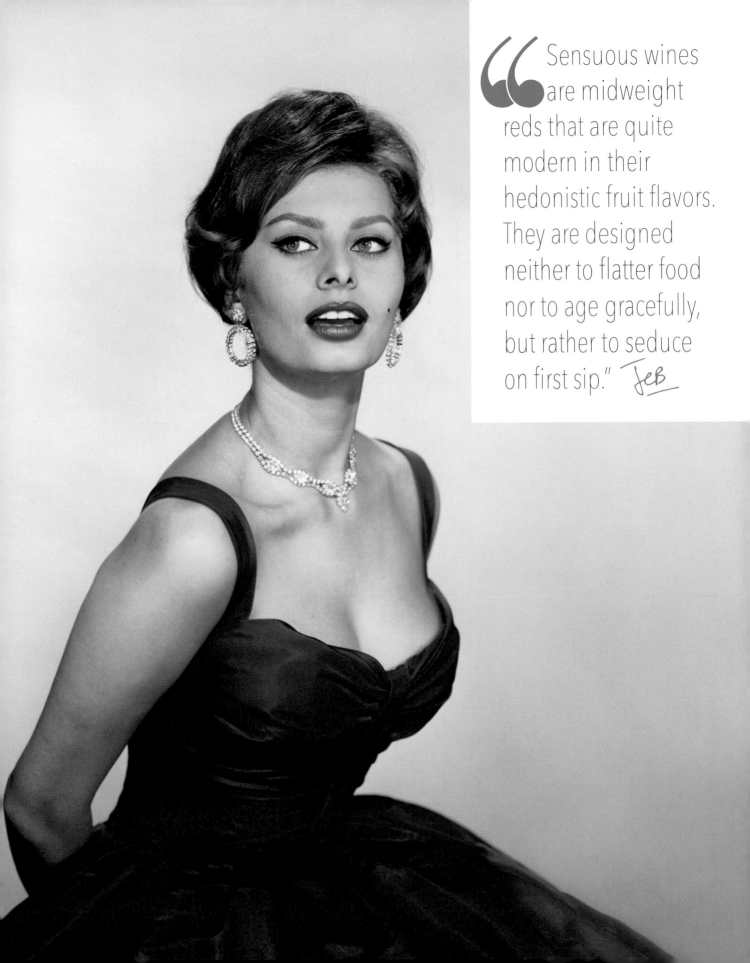

> "Sensuous wines are midweight reds that are quite modern in their hedonistic fruit flavors. They are designed neither to flatter food nor to age gracefully, but rather to seduce on first sip." *JeB*

SENSUOUS REDS
EASY-DRINKING RED WINES FOR ANY OCCASION

Warm climates and delayed harvesting are ideal for making these pleasingly plump reds since high degrees of ripeness are needed. The result is lip-smacking flavors of ripe red and black fruit, often with a candied or dessert-like aromatic character.

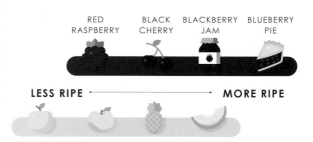

RED RASPBERRY   BLACK CHERRY   BLACKBERRY JAM   BLUEBERRY PIE

LESS RIPE ⟶ MORE RIPE

“Plush, satisfying, indulgent—Sensuous wines are the drinker's equivalent of comfort food. They warm the heart, soothe the senses, and recapture a taste of lost innocence.” *Jeb*

1   2   3   4   5

1   BOUCHARD AÎNÉ & FILS
    BEAUJOLAIS-VILLAGES

2   MOMMESSIN—LES GRANDES MISES
    ST. AMOUR—CRU DE BEAUJOLAIS

3   JCB NO. 7
    SONOMA COAST PINOT NOIR

4   BUENA VISTA WINERY
    PRIVATE RESERVE PINOT NOIR

5   DE LOACH VINEYARDS—O.F.S.
    RUSSIAN RIVER VALLEY PINOT NOIR

6   BUENA VISTA WINERY
    THE COUNT RED BLEND

7   DE LOACH VINEYARDS
    FORGOTTEN VINES ZINFANDEL

8   RAYMOND VINEYARDS
    NAPA VALLEY MERLOT

9   LYETH—MERITAGE
    SONOMA COUNTY RED WINE

10 TAROT
    NAPA VALLEY CABERNET SAUVIGNON

HEAVIER WEIGHT

LIGHTER WEIGHT

MILDER FLAVOR   BOLDER FLAVOR

This flavor map shows how Vivacious wines relate to one another by charting them according to two of wine's key intensity scales. Lighter to heavier weight refers to wine's texture and is loosely analogous to alcohol content in dry wines. Milder to bolder flavor refers to wine's overall flavor impact, which includes both fruit and oak flavors. Neither metric can capture the complexity and length of finish that are the hallmarks of quality in wine, of course, but they can be useful for navigating style options and for pairing wines with different foods.

6   7   8   9   10

POWERFUL REDS
HEAVYWEIGHT WINES OF INTENSITY

inky   mouth-filling
concentrated   structured

POWERFUL
DARK, BOLD, &
ASSERTIVELY OAKED

● tannic grip   ▲ low-yield
▬ barrel-spiced   ◐ age-worthy

HIGH TANNINS   HIGH ALCOHOL   HIGH OAK FLAVOR

PREMIUM CALIFORNIA RED BLENDS

CALIFORNIA CABERNET SAUVIGNON

PREMIUM CALIFORNIA ZINFANDEL

WHAT DISTINGUISHES POWERFUL WINES?

The Intensity Factor—Powerful wines are incredibly concentrated: they're dark in color, high in alcohol, and bold in flavors of both fruit and oak. Their attack features a classic one-two punch that lovers of big reds adore, leading with gobs of blackberry and cherry fruit and finishing with a lasting, vanilla-spiced resonance worthy of great Cognac or Bourbon.

High Grape Ripeness—Since thick-skinned grapes need ample sunshine and warmth to reach their potential for color and flavor, Powerful wines can only be made from fully ripe grapes in relatively warm regions. However, if they are to resist oxidation during barrel-aging, these grapes must be harvested before their acidity and tannins soften completely. As a result, they feature higher alcohol, higher tannins, and more overt oak flavor than other reds. These components cry out for foods high in protein, fat, and salt—like steakhouse fare—and can overwhelm foods that are less rich or served raw. Powerful wines often fall flat when paired with dishes high in acidity, sugar, or spicy heat.

Age-Worthy Structure—Powerful wines need high acidity and high tannins—both components are essential if wine is to improve with age, first in barrels at the winery and then in bottles in the cellar.

"Powerful is an audacious style that includes our most assertive reds from grapes like Cabernet Sauvignon, aged long-term in new oak barrels." *JeB*

POWERFUL REDS
POTENT, AGE-WORTHY RED WINES OF SUBSTANCE

Prime vineyards with sunny days and cool nights are required for making these denser wines since they need plenty of sun-driven color, flavor, and alcohol, yet can't risk losing their ability to deliver balancing acidity and freshness. Black fruit flavors of liqueur-like intensity dominate.

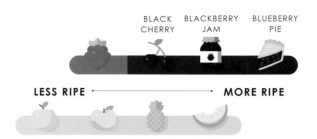

BLACK CHERRY   BLACKBERRY JAM   BLUEBERRY PIE

LESS RIPE ⟶ MORE RIPE

" Charismatic, noble, profound—Powerful wines are conquerors. They rise to every occasion, command our attention, and leave us desiring more." *JeB*

1   2   3   4   5

1 FORTANT
   HERITAGE COLLECTION RED BLEND

2 BUENA VISTA WINERY
   THE SHERIFF RED BLEND

3 BUENA VISTA WINERY
   PRIVATE RESERVE ZINFANDEL

4 RAYMOND VINEYARDS—RESERVE
   NAPA VALLEY CABERNET SAUVIGNON

5 JCB—PASSION
   NAPA VALLEY RED BLEND

6 LVE—LEGEND VINEYARDS EXCLUSIVE
   NAPA VALLEY CABERNET SAUVIGNON

7 CHATEAU BUENA VISTA
   NAPA VALLEY CABERNET SAUVIGNON

8 RAYMOND—GENERATIONS
   NAPA VALLEY CABERNET SAUVIGNON

9 JCB NO. 10
   NAPA VALLEY CABERNET SAUVIGNON

10 THE SURREALIST BY JCB
   NAPA VALLEY RED WINE

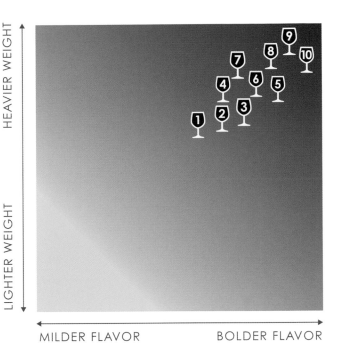

HEAVIER WEIGHT

LIGHTER WEIGHT

MILDER FLAVOR   BOLDER FLAVOR

This flavor map shows how Vivacious wines relate to one another by charting them according to two of wine's key intensity scales. Lighter to heavier weight refers to wine's texture and is loosely analogous to alcohol content in dry wines. Milder to bolder flavor refers to wine's overall flavor impact, which includes both fruit and oak flavors. Neither metric can capture the complexity and length of finish that are the hallmarks of quality in wine, of course, but they can be useful for navigating style options and for pairing wines with different foods.

6   7   8   9   10

CHAPTER

THE NOBLE
GRAPE VARIETIES
WINE'S KEY INGREDIENTS

Hundreds of grapes are used in making wine, but only a handful are worth learning about and remembering. These are the world's finest wine grapes, such as Chardonnay, Pinot Noir, and Cabernet Sauvignon, which have earned their celebrity status by their quality and popularity with wine drinkers, Since fine wine was pioneered in France, most of these "rock star" grapes are of French heritage, but they are now truly international and are cultivated around the globe.

VITIS VINIFERA
THE ONE & ONLY WINE GRAPE SPECIES

Grapes come in a wide a range of colors, flavors, and shapes—just as heirloom tomatoes and apples do—but all fine wine grapes are members of a single species called *vitis vinifera*. Native to Eurasia, *vitis vinifera* has been domesticated for at least 8,000 years, not only for making wine but also to be eaten fresh or dried.

Grapevines are not grown from seed; rather, they're "cloned" by planting cuttings taken from an established vine. When cultivating grapes, growers will always take cuttings from those plants with the most desirable traits. In a quality-oriented region like France, those might be a deep color or an excellent flavor. In a region more focused on volume, those desired traits might simply be generous crops and an overall suitability for the local climate. Either way, the result is that after millennia of cloning, the domesticated *vitis vinifera* vine is prone to genetic mutation. This has resulted in thousands of different "cultivars," or grape varieties, each with their own distinctive characteristics.

Each individual grape variety is native to a particular region of Europe, with the densest concentration of native grapes found in the places with the most intensive winemaking cultures, such as France, Italy, Spain, and Greece. These grapes may be planted and propagated elsewhere, of course, now that winemaking is a global enterprise that extends beyond the classic wine regions of Europe. However, international demand is strongest for those grapes capable of making the finest wines—grapes with the longest history of quality and the strongest track record of performance in new and diverse regions. As a result, the vast majority of wine grapes planted in places like California are of French origin, rather than of Italian, Spanish, or Greek origin.

WHY GRAPES?

No other fruit can compete with grapes in terms of the sweetness of its juice, which translates directly to potential alcohol after fermentation. High alcohol acts as a natural preservative, suppressing the types of bacterial and fungal spoilage that can quickly compromise other foods and drinks. Wine grapes are sweeter than table grapes and can easily produce wine with 10% to 15% alcohol. Apples are the next most viable choice, but since they are both less sweet and less juicy than grapes, ciders typically contain only 4% to 8% alcohol.

ORANGE	APPLE	TABLE GRAPE	WINE GRAPE
9%	**13%**	**16%**	**22%**
SUGAR	SUGAR	SUGAR	SUGAR

Wine grapes are bred for traits that help winemakers, like higher sugar content and thicker skins, while table grapes have firmer flesh and smaller seeds.

"Grapes offer the sweetest of all fruit juices, and, therefore, produce the most potent of all fermented drinks." JeB

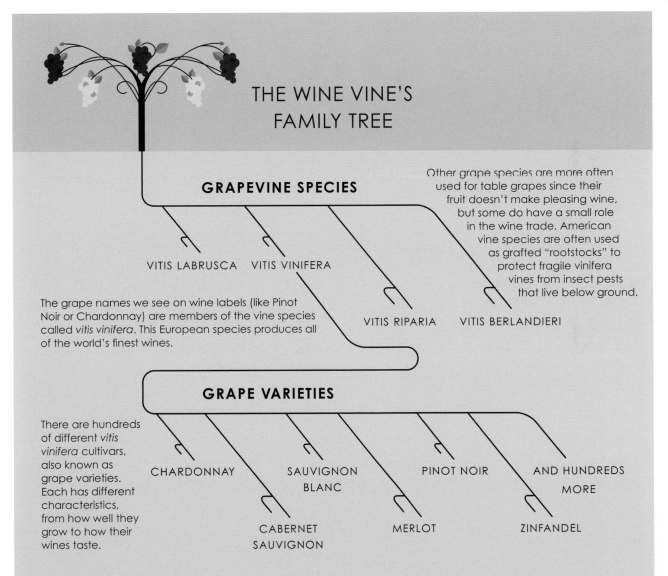

THE WINE VINE'S FAMILY TREE

GRAPEVINE SPECIES

Other grape species are more often used for table grapes since their fruit doesn't make pleasing wine, but some do have a small role in the wine trade. American vine species are often used as grafted "rootstocks" to protect fragile vinifera vines from insect pests that live below ground.

VITIS LABRUSCA   VITIS VINIFERA

The grape names we see on wine labels (like Pinot Noir or Chardonnay) are members of the vine species called *vitis vinifera*. This European species produces all of the world's finest wines.

VITIS RIPARIA   VITIS BERLANDIERI

GRAPE VARIETIES

There are hundreds of different *vitis vinifera* cultivars, also known as grape varieties. Each has different characteristics, from how well they grow to how their wines taste.

CHARDONNAY   SAUVIGNON BLANC   PINOT NOIR   AND HUNDREDS MORE

CABERNET SAUVIGNON   MERLOT   ZINFANDEL

Many noble grape varieties (such as Pinot Noir) are low-bearing vines that don't produce heavy crops and need very specific growing conditions to thrive. Others (like Chardonnay) are far more adaptable to varying geography, while some varieties (such as Zinfandel) are "workhorse grapes" that are capable of producing far higher volumes of grapes.

THE LEADING FINE WINE GRAPES
UNIFORMLY FRENCH IN ORIGIN, BUT DIVERSE IN FLAVOR

The traditional way to organize grape varieties is according to their native region: Chardonnay is a "Burgundy grape," while Merlot is a "Bordeaux grape." Because French vintners were selecting vines for their quality potential, rather than their productivity potential, centuries before their nearest rivals began doing so, French winemakers ensured that French grapes would come to rule the wine world. Naturally, when New World vintners wanted to improve their wines in the nineteenth century, they imported cuttings of French grapevines. As demand for better wines increased in the twentieth century, vintners with their own native grapes in other regions of Europe, like Italy and Spain, also started to plant French vines for the same reason.

> "Grapes from the same region are often related; some share a family resemblance as well as their lineage." *JeB*

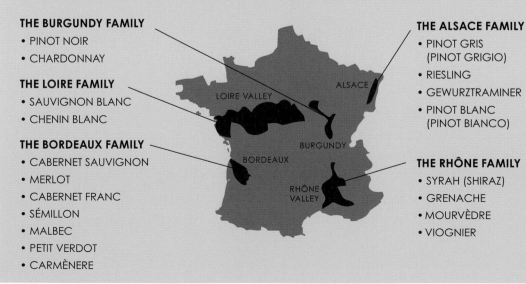

FRANCE'S ROYAL FAMILIES OF FINE WINE GRAPES

Grapes native to five of France's wine zones dominate the world's quality-oriented vineyards. The top two have global name recognition as fine wine regions: Burgundy is the point of origin of Pinot Noir and Chardonnay, and Bordeaux is home to Cabernet Sauvignon and Merlot. Three more wine regions—the Rhône Valley, the Loire Valley, and Alsace—may be less well known to the general public, but these regions loom large in the wine trade as being the native regions of grapes like Syrah (Shiraz), Sauvignon Blanc, and Riesling.

THE BURGUNDY FAMILY
- PINOT NOIR
- CHARDONNAY

THE LOIRE FAMILY
- SAUVIGNON BLANC
- CHENIN BLANC

THE BORDEAUX FAMILY
- CABERNET SAUVIGNON
- MERLOT
- CABERNET FRANC
- SÉMILLON
- MALBEC
- PETIT VERDOT
- CARMÈNERE

THE ALSACE FAMILY
- PINOT GRIS (PINOT GRIGIO)
- RIESLING
- GEWURZTRAMINER
- PINOT BLANC (PINOT BIANCO)

THE RHÔNE FAMILY
- SYRAH (SHIRAZ)
- GRENACHE
- MOURVÈDRE
- VIOGNIER

ALSACE

LOIRE VALLEY

BURGUNDY

BORDEAUX

RHÔNE VALLEY

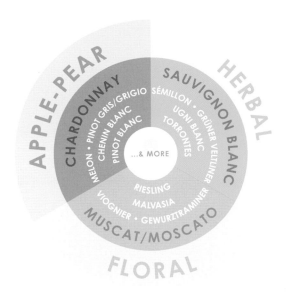

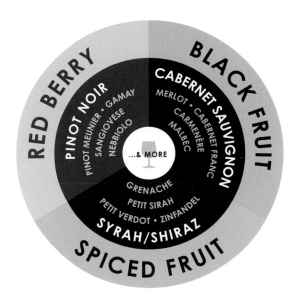

GROUPING WINE GRAPES INTO FLAVOR FAMILIES

Knowing which region a grape comes from is certainly useful for navigating wine lists and retail shelves, but it can be more helpful to classify grapes according to sensory qualities, particularly similarities in their overall flavor and scent.

Among white wines, there is a broad apple-pear resemblance between wines made from most grape varieties, like Chardonnay and Pinot Gris (also known as Pinot Grigio). The subtlety of these styles makes them quite food-friendly and popular. A few green-skinned grapes stand out, however, because they have aromatics that are stronger and more distinctive, like the leafy green scent of Sauvignon Blanc or the effusive floral perfume of Muscat (also known as Moscato).

Despite their higher flavor intensity compared to white grapes, red grapes can be harder to categorize aromatically. While white wines have simpler scents that are derived from compounds present in the fresh grapes, reds gain more aromatic complexity during fermentation (and most also feature a layer of oak flavors). However, red wine grapes can be sorted into broad families, too.

Most red wines smell of fruits with deep colors. Grapes that thrive in cool climates, like Pinot Noir or Gamay, taste most like the brightest red berries, featuring scents reminiscent of strawberries, raspberries, or cherries. Many red grapes that prefer warmer zones make wines that smell and taste more of darker, almost-black fruits, like blackberries or blueberries, as seen with Cabernet Sauvignon and Merlot. Some warm-climate red grapes also feature an unusual concentration of exotic, non-fruit scents—appetizing aromas of black pepper or cocoa, for example. Since wines from grapes like Syrah and Grenache can smell like they've been seasoned from the spice rack, we'll call this the spiced fruit family.

PINOT NOIR
THE LEGENDARY RED GRAPE OF BURGUNDY

Considered by many to be the world's most noble wine variety, Pinot Noir is also the most delicate of the famous red grapes. Pinot Noir clusters look just as dark as Cabernet on the vine, but their thinner skins are more fragile and yield wines that are lighter in color and the very definition of *finesse*. Although Pinot Noir's seductive scent is its greatest asset, it can be difficult to describe. Top Pinot Noir wines often smell oddly funky, evoking wild mushrooms or artisanal cheeses as much as they do traditional red fruits and berries.

> "Pinot Noir is a gift of God and there is something addictively sensual about its wines. They capture the magic of life and speak directly to the soul."
>
> *JeB*

Pinot Noir also is a rarity among dark grapes in that it prefers cooler climates—if it gets too ripe, its wines lose their magic, so the finest Pinot Noirs tend to be lighter and more acidic than other reds. Even when it is made with a modest level of ambition, though, Pinot Noir's remarkable affinity for food and lively flavors has turned a generation of wine drinkers onto the joys of drinking lighter, brighter red wines.

PINOT NOIR | THE SENSORY PROFILE

AROMATIC FAMILY

RED BERRY · BLACK FRUIT · SPICED FRUIT

PREFERS COOL CLIMATES

DISTINCTIVE EARTHY FLAVORS

VERY HIGH ACIDITY

STRAWBERRY

POMEGRANATE

RASPBERRY

CHERRY

FLAVOR RANGE BY RIPENESS

 LOW RIPENESS/COOL CLIMATE

HIGH RIPENESS/WARM CLIMATE

ORIGINS

Pinot Noir is one of the wine world's most ancient grape varieties. Some evidence suggests it was being cultivated in Burgundy as early as the fourth century, but written records under its modern name would not appear for another thousand years. Its incredible age and tendency to mutate help explain why Pinot Noir appears in the genetic family tree of so many fine wine grapes, from Chardonnay to Cabernet Sauvignon to Syrah.

Pinot Noir is the sole red grape grown in Burgundy (save only the Beaujolais district, where growers cultivate a lighter, fruitier descendant of Pinot called Gamay). Pinot Noir's uncanny knack for tasting slightly different wherever it is grown was first explored in the late Middle Ages, when it was noted that each aspect of a vineyard's terrain—from soil type to slope to sun exposure—could create a recognizable flavor "fingerprint." This concept came to be known as *terroir,* which is a French term for "earth." Many of the modern wine world's core principles are based on the terroir-centric methodology pioneered in Burgundy. Of these, the most important is the location-based hierarchy of wine appellations, which makes wine labels so disorienting.

HOW FRENCH PINOT NOIR INSPIRED THE MODERN WINE LABELING SYSTEM

Centuries ago, it was observed that red Burgundy wines grown in different vineyards tasted different and varied in their quality potential. As a result, Pinot Noirs from the finest sites came to be bottled separately and named for their vineyards, while grapes from less-distinguished sites were blended together for practicality. The blends were also named for their place of origin: the best were named for their village or "commune," the next-best for their district, and then the next level for their larger region, etc., always in decreasing order of quality and, therefore, selling price.

VINEYARD $$$$
★★★★

VILLAGE $$$
★★★

DISTRICT $$
★★

REGION $
★

Today, all wine labels use this Burgundian principle. A mandatory region-of-origin statement or "appellation" indicates where the grapes were grown. The least ambitious wines are the least specific about where their grapes come from, while the finest wines are the most specific. Although this system makes perfect sense, it does complicate matters for wine lovers. The appellations of the cheapest wines will always have the greatest name recognition because they are named for giant regions of global importance, like California or Burgundy. However, the finest wines are always named for much smaller places that most people have never heard of, like the obscure Carneros district of Sonoma or the tiny hamlet of Vougeot.

CHARDONNAY
THE GREAT WHITE GRAPE OF BURGUNDY

No other white grape can rival the quality potential of Chardonnay or its exceptional popularity with wine drinkers. Since the vine adapts remarkably well to a dizzying array of climate conditions, every country that produces wine grows at least a little Chardonnay.

Compared to other white grapes, Chardonnay has an unusual capacity to deliver seductive texture at radically different degrees of ripeness, thus producing world-class wines in both the coldest and warmest wine regions.

> "Chardonnay is a marvel—it can make exceptionally rich white wines without losing finesse, yet also produce ephemerally delicate wines without lacking substance." *JeB*

TAKE CHARDONNAY'S TEMPERATURE

Chardonnay's greatest weakness is its relatively neutral flavor, so vintners rarely leave it unadorned, choosing instead to amplify its aromatics in the winemaking process. Just as a chef might use herbs or spices in a recipe, winemakers can age Chardonnay in contact with a flavor source, adding either the Cognac-like taste of new oak barrels or the more subtle bread-dough flavor of wine's natural "lees" or yeast sediments.

PURE CHARDONNAY FLAVORS

Warm but breezy vineyards
UNOAKED CALIFORNIA CHARDONNAY (modest)
Grapes of high-ish ripeness make midweight wines with moderate acidity and fresh tropical fruit flavors. (Think fresh pineapple.)

Cold vineyards
FRENCH CHABLIS
Grapes of very low ripeness make light- to midweight wines with high acidity and subtle fruit flavors. (Think fresh green apples.)

CHARDONNAY + OAK FLAVORS

Warmest vineyards
NAPA VALLEY CHARDONNAY (premium)
Grapes of very high ripeness make heavyweight wines with modest acidity, baked fruit flavor, and overt oak accents. (Think apple pie with a scoop of butter-pecan ice cream.)

Cool but sunny vineyards
FRENCH MEURSAULT
Grapes of low-ish ripeness make midweight wines with high acidity, mild fruit flavors, and noticeable oak accents. (Think fresh golden apples and roasted hazelnuts.)

CHARDONNAY + YEAST FLAVORS

Coldest vineyards
FRENCH CHAMPAGNE OR CRÉMANT
Underripe grapes make very lightweight wines with very high acidity, sour fruit flavors, and subtle yeasty accents. (Think sour apples or rhubarb and French toast.)

ORIGINS

Chardonnay originated in France's Burgundy region, where it was first mentioned in the records of Cistercian monks in the year 1330. DNA research has revealed Chardonnay's parent vines to be Burgundy's legendary red grape Pinot Noir and a more resilient white grape called Gouais Blanc. This was a heavenly match—it seems that Chardonnay inherited Pinot Noir's expressiveness and potential for quality without falling heir to that grape's fragility and low productivity.

By the eighteenth century, Chardonnay came to dominate the white wines of Burgundy; now, it's propagated worldwide. In France, all white wines from Burgundy are made with Chardonnay grapes in practice, although some others are still permitted under Burgundian law. Classy and understated, white Burgundy is the benchmark for Chardonnay wines, emulated by vintners around the globe regardless of whether it's being made in a subtle unoaked style as it is in Mâcon-Villages or if it's being made in the nuttier oaked style of great wines such as Meursault. However, Chardonnay has another iconic role as the backbone of France's finest sparkling wines. When planted in warmer New World regions, like California's Sonoma County, Chardonnay makes both still and sparkling wines of a similar stylistic range, just with the added boost of more sunshine and warmth. This results in stronger, fruitier wines with richer texture and lower acidity. Most of these wines display the grape's name on the label.

CHARDONNAY | THE SENSORY PROFILE

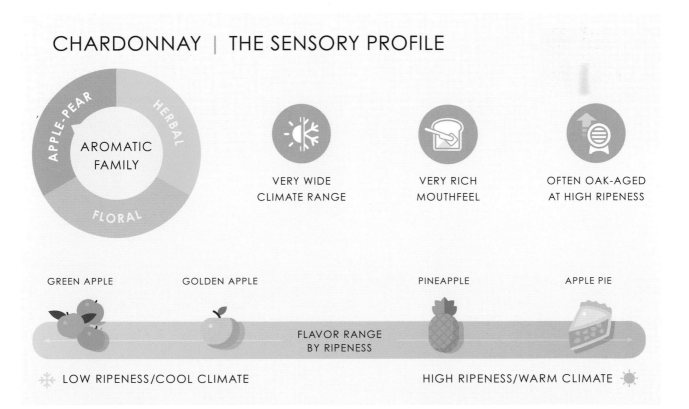

CABERNET SAUVIGNON
THE SUPERSTAR RED GRAPE OF NAPA VALLEY & BORDEAUX

Cabernet Sauvignon grapes are unusually small and have very thick skins. Once crushed for fermentation, this results in a higher proportion of grape solids to grape juice, yielding wines of a very dark color and a very strong flavor. They also contain unusually high levels of the three main components necessary for red wines to age gracefully: tannins, alcohol, and acidity. As a result, Cabernet Sauvignon makes some of the world's finest reds and is often used as a blending ingredient to intensify and "improve" wines made from less formidable grapes.

> "Cabernet Sauvignon has great power—it is a true wonder of nature. The sheer force of its tannins and acidity can preserve its freshness and beauty for decades." *JeB*

Cabernet Sauvignon's thick skins do mean that the grapes require ample sunshine and warmth to ripen fully and develop balanced flavors. When pruned back to reduce crop volume and aged long-term in oak barrels, the grapes make truly impressive wines—inky heavyweights of great concentration. But Cabernet Sauvignon rarely performs as well when farmed for volume at the bargain level.

CABERNET SAUVIGNON | THE ULTIMATE BLENDING GRAPE

Since Cabernet Sauvignon makes dark, concentrated wines, it is often used to deepen and darken blends. In most countries, wines must only contain 75% to 85% of a given grape variety to carry that name on their label. This means many wines that contain Cabernet Sauvignon make no mention of it on the label, while others labeled as Cabernet Sauvignon may be made with less than 100% of that variety.

LABELED AS BORDEAUX OR BLENDS
French Bordeaux almost never contains more than 75% Cabernet Sauvignon; most contain less than 15%. Modest Merlot-based wines use small amounts to add needed color, weight, and flavor, but even in premium Cabernet-based wines, the main ingredient is softened with milder grapes. Many of the world's finest red wines follow this "Cabernet-based" recipe but may not name Cabernet Sauvignon on the label.

LABELED AS CABERNET SAUVIGNON
It is more common to label wines by their grape variety in New World regions like the Americas. Cabernet Sauvignon is also more pleasant and less harsh when grown in warmer, sunnier places like California. As a result, American wine drinkers encounter far more wines labeled as Cabernet Sauvignon. However, many of these remain blends, just with no more than 25% of other varieties added.

ORIGINS

Cabernet Sauvignon is native to the Bordeaux region. It may be the world's most-planted wine grape and is considered by many to be the world's finest wine grape, but in terms of history, its age of fewer than 600 years makes it a relative newcomer. Recent genetic studies of this grape revealed, rather surprisingly, that its name accurately identifies its parentage: it's the offspring of two much older varieties cultivated in Bordeaux, namely Cabernet Franc and Sauvignon Blanc.

Cabernet Sauvignon is the Bordeaux region's most famous grape and is the backbone of the legendary wines of Bordeaux's "Left Bank." However, it is not even close to being Bordeaux's primary grape in terms of how widely it's planted—that title belongs to its sibling, Merlot (see next page). Why? Cabernet Sauvignon requires more sun and warmth to ripen than what most of Bordeaux's terrain can offer. It can only ripen properly in the deep beds of dry gravel flanking the estuary, most notably in the districts of Médoc and Graves. However, where it does ripen, it can boost wine quality significantly and tends to represent 50% to 75% of the blends in those areas. When Bordeaux's top wines were assessed for inclusion in the 1855 World's Fair in Paris, all fifty-five Châteaux so honored were located in Médoc or Graves and were making Cabernet Sauvignon-based blends. Cabernet Sauvignon's nobility has led it to be widely planted worldwide, most notably in California's Napa Valley, where it can ripen much more easily.

CABERNET SAUVIGNON | THE SENSORY PROFILE

AROMATIC FAMILY

RED BERRY · BLACK FRUIT · SPICED FRUIT

PREFERS WARM CLIMATES

VERY HIGH COLOR & FLAVOR INTENSITY

VERY HIGH TANNIN

ROASTED PEPPER

BLACK CURRANT

BLACKBERRY

BRANDIED CHERRY

FLAVOR RANGE BY RIPENESS

❄ LOW RIPENESS/COOL CLIMATE

HIGH RIPENESS/WARM CLIMATE ☀

MERLOT & THE BLENDING GRAPES
THE SUPPORTING RED GRAPES OF BORDEAUX BLENDS

MERLOT

The most widely planted grape of the Bordeaux region and the second most planted in Napa Valley, Merlot is a half-sibling to Cabernet Sauvignon that makes softer, fruitier wines. Merlot has larger grapes that ripen earlier, making it the more economically viable variety of the two to grow. Merlot wines offer generous helpings of dark berry flavors and a luscious mouthfeel. These tend to be a touch lighter and paler than Cabernet Sauvignon, with softer tannins and milder acidity. Such traits make Merlot much more enjoyable to drink when young but less well-suited to long-term cellar aging. Indeed, Merlot is so crowd-pleasing that it is frequently exploited for volume in everyday wines. Such cheap and cheerful Merlot wines may have devalued the grape's reputation for quality to some degree, but when planted in top vineyard sites and made in adherence to rigorous standards, Merlot makes wines of incredible power and grace.

> " Merlot is Cabernet Sauvignon's softer, more velvety sibling. This alluring grape ranks among the very finest in the world." *Jeb*

MERLOT | THE SENSORY PROFILE

AROMATIC FAMILY

RED BERRY

BLACK FRUIT

SPICED FRUIT

WIDE CLIMATE RANGE

VERY HIGH IN FRUITY FLAVORS

LOWER THAN AVERAGE TANNIN

TOMATO

BLACK PLUM

FLAVOR RANGE BY RIPENESS

BLACKBERRY

CHERRY PIE

❄ LOW RIPENESS/COOL CLIMATE

HIGH RIPENESS/WARM CLIMATE ☀

CABERNET FRANC

This most ancient of Bordeaux vines is responsible for the family resemblance in the flavors of the top two Bordeaux grapes since it is a parent to both Cabernet Sauvignon and Merlot. It is often derided as "Cabernet Light" because its wines tend to be lighter and paler and also milder and more acidic than its more-famous relation. However, Cabernet Franc can make wines of stunning complexity and character when given prime vineyard sites and treated with respect. That said, it is more often encountered as a minor blending ingredient—typically less than 10%—that adds bright acidity along with its signature forest flavors of wild berries and cedar.

PETIT VERDOT

Petit Verdot's name means "small green" because its thick-skinned grapes are quite slow to ripen. Very little is grown in Bordeaux, where it's used only occasionally in tiny amounts to add color and tannin to blends. This grape is experiencing a revival of interest in warmer regions like California, where it can yield inky, floral-scented reds of great power.

MALBEC

Malbec shares a parent with Merlot and is also native to southwestern France. It is a permitted ingredient in Bordeaux wines and was once used to add color and tannin to Merlot-based blends. However, at this point, very little Malbec is cultivated in Bordeaux—it simply needs a warmer, sunnier climate to ripen fully. Malbec has now found its climate in Argentina, where it is the country's dominant grape.

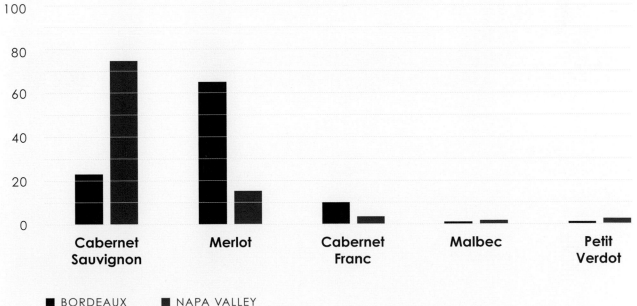

PLANTED AREA OF RED BORDEAUX GRAPES
COMPARISON BY PERCENTAGE OF TOTAL

■ BORDEAUX ■ NAPA VALLEY

Relative Percentage of Vineyard Area, Counting Only Red Bordeaux Grapes

SAUVIGNON BLANC (& SÉMILLON)
THE WHITE GRAPES OF BORDEAUX

Sauvignon Blanc makes wines with a fragrance that is more powerful than that of most white wines. The grape's name shares the same root as "savage" in English, although it's unclear whether this refers to the wine's fierce scent or to its resemblance to an untamed vine. Sauvignon Blanc grapes contain more acidity and less sugar at full ripeness than Chardonnay grapes do, producing wines that are lighter and more refreshing. Its aromatics tend toward the green end of the flavor spectrum, reminiscent not only of green fruits, like lime, kiwi, or honeydew melon, but also of more savory green foods, like parsley, pickles, or snow peas.

> "Sauvignon Blanc has a distinctive, spontaneous, and crisp personality. Few wines have a perfume as citrusy or as evocative of green herbs." *Jeb*

One of Sauvignon Blanc's great strengths is that it is unusually cost-efficient—the vine can tolerate cool, damp climates and still deliver bumper crops of flavorful fruit. Stylistically, it is most often cold-fermented and sold immediately, without any barrel-aging. Both factors lead to delightful wines at very popular prices.

SAUVIGNON BLANC | THE SENSORY PROFILE

AROMATIC FAMILY

APPLE-PEAR

HERBAL

FLORAL

PREFERS COOL CLIMATES

UNUSUALLY GREEN LEAFY FLAVORS

VERY HIGH ACIDITY

GREEN APPLE

GRAPEFRUIT

PASSION FRUIT

KIWI FRUIT

FLAVOR RANGE BY RIPENESS

 LOW RIPENESS/COOL CLIMATE

HIGH RIPENESS/WARM CLIMATE ☀

ORIGINS

Sauvignon Blanc is an ancient French grape and a distant descendant of Pinot Noir. Recent research has shown that it originated in the northern part of France's Loire Valley, a region famous for producing dry whites like Sancerre and Pouilly-Fumé. Indeed, when Sauvignon Blanc is grown elsewhere, its wines most often follow the refreshing style popularized in the Loire, where it is always unoaked and unblended. However, Sauvignon Blanc has also been grown in Bordeaux for centuries. There, it's occasionally barrel-fermented and is almost always blended with other grapes, most notably Sémillon. In white Bordeaux blends, Sauvignon Blanc dominates the dry wines and is found under appellations like Graves and Entre-Deux-Mers, while the thinner-skinned Sémillon takes the lead in sweet dessert wines, such as the legendary late-harvested Sauternes.

SÉMILLON

Sémillon has been Sauvignon Blanc's white Bordeaux sidekick for so long (and shares so many traits when fermented dry) that it's easy to assume the two grapes are local siblings. However, recent DNA studies have shown Sémillon to be much more closely related to the Loire Valley's main white grape, Chenin Blanc—which similarly excels at sweet wines—than it is to Sauvignon Blanc, suggesting that Sémillon also hails from the Loire. Depending on ripeness, Sémillon wines can range from tart and lemony to honeyed and fig-like.

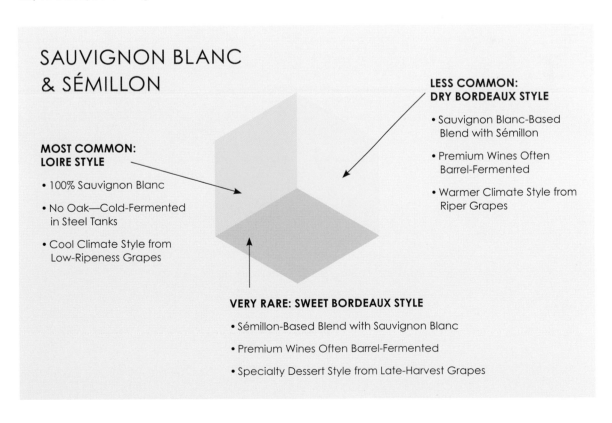

SAUVIGNON BLANC & SÉMILLON

LESS COMMON:
DRY BORDEAUX STYLE

- Sauvignon Blanc-Based Blend with Sémillon
- Premium Wines Often Barrel-Fermented
- Warmer Climate Style from Riper Grapes

MOST COMMON:
LOIRE STYLE

- 100% Sauvignon Blanc
- No Oak—Cold-Fermented in Steel Tanks
- Cool Climate Style from Low-Ripeness Grapes

VERY RARE: SWEET BORDEAUX STYLE

- Sémillon-Based Blend with Sauvignon Blanc
- Premium Wines Often Barrel-Fermented
- Specialty Dessert Style from Late-Harvest Grapes

GRENACHE & SYRAH
THE RED GRAPES OF THE RHÔNE VALLEY & SOUTH OF FRANCE

ORIGINS

Many grapes are grown in the Rhône Valley of southern France, but only Grenache and Syrah have become internationally renowned. The vast majority of Rhône wines are blended. Most are Grenache-based blends with some Syrah added as a flavorful accent, a style associated with the southern Rhône Valley. Syrah dominates only the red wines of the colder, steeper slopes of the northern Rhône.

Technically, Grenache is the Spanish Garnacha grape but is much better known by its French name and Rhône heritage since it has been grown there for centuries. Grenache dominates Rhône vineyards and the region's most popular reds, from Côtes-du-Rhône to Châteauneuf-du-Pape. Syrah's roots have long been debated, but recent studies show it to be native to northern Rhône, where it makes famed wines like Hermitage and Côte-Rôtie. While they are known as "Rhône grapes," both Grenache and Syrah are also cultivated in other regions of the South of France, such as Provence, the Languedoc, and Roussillon.

GRENACHE | THE SENSORY PROFILE

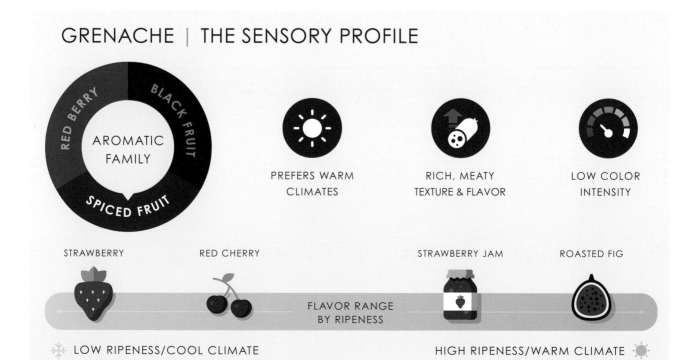

GRENACHE

Until quite recently, Grenache was the world's most-planted wine grape, but it was very rarely named on wine labels. The ultimate "workhorse" grape, Grenache is popular with winegrowers because of its freakish ability to produce huge volumes of grapes per vine without the dilution of flavor that normally accompanies heavy crop yields. When it is pruned back, Grenache can make big, meaty red wines of nobility and substance. However, since Grenache wines look paler and oxidize faster than most reds, it is most often supplemented with dollops of two darker Rhône grapes, Syrah and Mourvèdre, a practice that has led many Rhône-inspired blends to be labeled "GSM" for short.

> "Spicy Grenache and Syrah dominate the South of France. They are the twin pillars of the region's wine heritage." *Jeb*

SYRAH

Syrah is a French grape whose wines have a distinctive inky purple color and flavors of black pepper and blackberries, but it's better known as Shiraz, the synonym it goes by in the southern hemisphere. With skins as thick as Cabernet Sauvignon, Syrah grapes need just as much sunshine to ripen fully and makes wines that are just as intense. As a result, Syrah is often similarly used to boost the color and flavor of lighter red wines (as it does in most "Rhône blends"). But Syrah is naturally fruitier than Cabernet Sauvignon, meaning it can more easily stand alone as a balanced wine. Stand-alone Syrah is most common in warmer, sunnier New World wine regions, like California and Australia.

SYRAH | THE SENSORY PROFILE

AROMATIC FAMILY

RED BERRY · BLACK FRUIT · SPICED FRUIT

PREFERS WARM CLIMATES

DISTINCTIVE PEPPERY FLAVOR

HIGH COLOR INTENSITY

RASPBERRY

BLACK PLUM

FLAVOR RANGE BY RIPENESS

BLACKBERRY JAM

BLUEBERRY PIE

❄ LOW RIPENESS/COOL CLIMATE

HIGH RIPENESS/WARM CLIMATE ☀

ZINFANDEL
THE HISTORIC RED GRAPE OF CALIFORNIA

Zinfandel produces strong red wines that feature a deep color and rustic flavors of dried fruit and pipe tobacco. Since the grape is often grown in warm regions and pushed toward very high degrees of ripeness, many of its wines are unusually high in alcohol and low in acidity. These traits can make wines taste a little sweeter than is typical for dry red wines; indeed, Zinfandel lends itself well to making both lightly sweet reds and fully sweet red dessert wines in the style of fortified Port. Zinfandel is a red grape, but in an ironic twist, it was popularized in the '80s as a lightly sweet "blush" wine under the name White Zinfandel.

Fans of the stronger red styles often seek out Zinfandels sourced from plots of so-called "old vines" that were planted before California's fine wine boom in the 1960s; these more mature vineyards are associated with greater flavor complexity. While there is no regulatory standard for this label statement, most Zinfandels labeled "Old Vines" come from vineyards that are thirty to one hundred years old.

> "Zinfandel is the only wine grape that California can truly call its own. It has proven its greatness and pedigree—not just in power, but in complexity and grace."
>
> *JeB*

WHY OLD VINES CAN IMPROVE WINE QUALITY

Grapevines can live for well over one hundred years, but as they grow older, they decline in vigor and produce fewer grapes. Therefore most vineyards are ripped out and replanted after twenty-five to forty years, when their productivity dips below the threshold of economic viability. Still, winemakers prize the fruit of older vineyards because of their resilience in poor weather and the superiority of their wines.

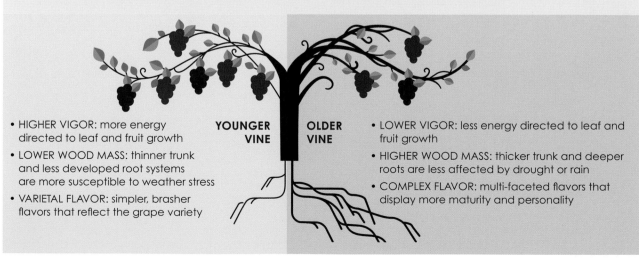

YOUNGER VINE

- HIGHER VIGOR: more energy directed to leaf and fruit growth
- LOWER WOOD MASS: thinner trunk and less developed root systems are more susceptible to weather stress
- VARIETAL FLAVOR: simpler, brasher flavors that reflect the grape variety

OLDER VINE

- LOWER VIGOR: less energy directed to leaf and fruit growth
- HIGHER WOOD MASS: thicker trunk and deeper roots are less affected by drought or rain
- COMPLEX FLAVOR: multi-faceted flavors that display more maturity and personality

ORIGINS

In the 1850s, Zinfandel was the first grape to prove truly successful for California's early winemakers: it adapted well to the terrain, yielded bumper crops, and made very good red wines. Within forty years, it became California's most-planted wine grape and remained so for another century. Many considered Zinfandel to be an American variety, in part because the Zinfandel name is used nowhere else in the world. The vine was clearly a European member of the *vitis vinifera* species, but its origins were unclear.

Recent genetic studies have finally traced Zinfandel's complex European heritage—it's a very ancient grape from Croatia's Dalmatian coast, where it goes by the names "Tribidrag" or "Crljenak Kaštelanski." It is no longer significantly cultivated there, but it is a minor crop in nearby southern Italy, where it is called "Primitivo."

So where did the name Zinfandel come from? Boston nurseries were selling "Black Zinfandel" in the early nineteenth century, which may have been a simple case of mislabeling. Cuttings of this vine were introduced to the United States from a botanical collection in what was then the Austrian Empire. An unrelated Austrian red grape now known as Blaufränkisch has historically appeared under a number of synonyms, including "Zierfahndler." Czech documents dating back as far as 1797 define a number of aliases for this same grape, including "Czilifant" and "Cinifadl." It seems likely that cuttings of Croatian Tribidrag in the Austrian collection may have been mistakenly tagged with a different grape's Czech nickname: Zinfandel.

ZINFANDEL | THE SENSORY PROFILE

RED BERRY
BLACK FRUIT
AROMATIC FAMILY
SPICED FRUIT

PREFERS WARM CLIMATES

VERY HIGH ALCOHOL

JAMMY FLAVORS (COOKED FRUIT)

STRAWBERRY

BING CHERRY

BLUEBERRY PIE

RUM RAISIN SUNDAE

FLAVOR RANGE BY RIPENESS

 LOW RIPENESS/COOL CLIMATE

HIGH RIPENESS/WARM CLIMATE

MORE WINE GRAPES
THE BEST OF THE REST

Beyond the top wine grapes featured on the previous pages, wine is made from dozens more grapes worldwide. That said, only a few have any significance outside their native region (see the grapes listed in this chart).

> " The wine grapes grown in the New World are almost all of French origin, but it is fascinating to discover the diversity of flavor found around the world." *JeB*

THE THREE SHADES OF GRAPE COLOR

Most white wines are made from green grapes, and all red wines are made from grapes that look blue-black on the vine. However, some purple grapes have a paler reddish hue and are routinely made into white wines, such as Gewurztraminer and Pinot Gris, better known as Pinot Grigio.

Recent DNA testing shows that the grapes known as Pinot Gris and Pinot Blanc are genetically identical to Pinot Noir, meaning that they are not separate vine varieties but are rather mutations of the original dark grape. How does this happen? Two genes determine color in grapes. When both are active, grapes are dark purple. When both are inactive, grapes are bright green. But if only one is active, the grapes will be purplish but with a dusty lavender hue.

GRAPE NAME	ALSO KNOWN AS
Albariño	Alvarinho
Aligoté	Blanc de Troyes, Chaudenet
Chenin Blanc	Steen
Colombard	Blanquette
Marsanne	
Melon	Muscadet, Gamay Blanc
Moscato	Muscat, Moscatel, Muskateller, Lexia
Pinot Blanc	Pinot Bianco, Weissburgunder
Riesling	
Viognier	
Gewurztraminer	Roter Traminer, Traminer Aromatico
Pinot Grigio	Pinot Gris, Pinot Beurot, Ruländ Malvoisie, Grauburgunder
Roussanne	Bergeron
Carignane	Carignano, Cariñena, Mazuelo Samsó
Charbono	Bonarda, Douce Noire
Cinsault	Black Malvoisie, Ottavianello, Hermitage
Gamay	
Mourvèdre	Monastrell, Mataro
Petite Sirah	Durif
Pinot Meunier	Müllerebe, Schwarzriesling
Sangiovese	Prugnolo Gentile, Morellino, Nielluccio
Tempranillo	Cencibel, Tinta Roriz, Aragonés
Valdiguié	Napa Gamay

REGION OF ORIGIN	OTHER KEY REGIONS	FLAVOR FAMILY	STYLE NOTES
Galicia, Spain	Northern Portugal, California	Apple-Pear	Lightweight with subtle fragrance. Never oaked.
Burgundy, France	Romania, Bulgaria, Russia, Ukraine	Apple-Pear	Lightweight with high acid and mild flavor. Never oaked.
Loire Valley, France	South Africa, California	Apple-Pear	Often sweet, but may also be dry & oaky in New World regions.
Southwest France	Cognac, California	Apple-Pear	Midweight with mild flavors. Rarely oaked.
Rhône Valley, France	Australia, California	Apple-Pear	Richly textured and nutty in flavor; may be barrel-fermented.
Burgundy, France	Loire Valley, Oregon	Apple-Pear	Lightweight with subtle flavor. Never oaked.
Greece	Italy, Spain, France, California, Australia	Floral	Usually sweet. Typically either semi-sparkling or fortified.
Burgundy, France	Northern Italy, Alsace, California, Germany	Apple-Pear	Italian-style: light & mild. French-style: richer & bolder.
Rhineland, Germany	Alsace, Northern Italy, Australia, New York	Apple-Pear	German-style: light & sweet. French-style: stronger & drier.
Rhône Valley, France	California, Australia	Floral	Richly textured and often barrel-fermented.
Rhineland, Germany	Alsace, California, New Zealand, Northern Italy	Floral	German-style: light & sweet. French-style: stronger & drier.
Burgundy, France	Northern Italy, Alsace, California, Oregon	Apple-Pear	Italian-style: light & mild. French-style: richer & bolder.
Rhône Valley, France	California	Herbal	Richly textured and slightly astringent; may be barrel-fermented.
Aragon, Spain	South of France, Italy, Rioja, Catalonia	Black Fruit	High acid and high tannin. Often used in blends.
Savoie, France	Argentina, California	Black Fruit	High acid and high tannin. Often used in blends.
Languedoc, France	Provence, Lebanon, California, South Africa	Black Fruit	Pale color and high acidity. Used mainly for light fruity reds and rosés.
Burgundy, France	Switzerland	Red Berry	Pale color and low tannin. Used mainly for light fruity reds.
Valencia, Spain	Rhône Valley, Provence, California, Australia	Spiced Fruit	Intense color and flavor. Often used as a booster in blends.
Languedoc, France	California, Australia	Spiced Fruit	Intense color and flavor. Often used as a booster in blends.
Burgundy, France	Champagne, California	Red Berry	Pale color. Used mainly for sparkling wines and rosé.
Tuscany, Italy	California, Australia, Sardinia	Red Berry	High acid and high tannin. Often used in blends.
Castille-Léon, Spain	Rioja, Castilla-La Mancha, California, Australia	Black Fruit	Versatile and midweight. Often used in blends.
Languedoc, France	California	Red Berry	Pale color. Often used in rosés.

CHAPTER *6*

THE ART OF WINE LIVING
HOME ENTERTAINING & PAIRING WITH FOOD

The beauty of wine is that this remarkable elixir can create emotions and stir passions, speaking with the ageless voice of the land. Wine is a living jewel, which by its nature allows us to appreciate things that lie beyond ourselves, both real and surreal. Wine doesn't simply enhance food and conversation; it enhances our appreciation of beauty, culture, ideas, sex, and even politics. Best of all, living the wine life reminds us to live each moment to the very fullest, wholly invested in the now.

ENTERTAINING WITH WINE
TIPS IN EVERYTHING FROM STORING TO POURING

Wine is a perishable product whose volatile components behave differently at different temperatures, affecting how it tastes and how well it keeps. Learning how these factors affect our enjoyment of wine makes it easier to predict how to maximize that enjoyment.

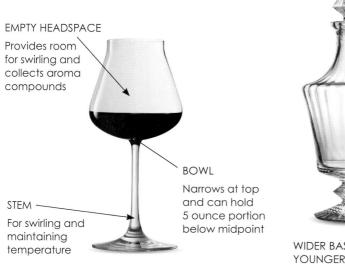

EMPTY HEADSPACE

Provides room for swirling and collects aroma compounds

BOWL

Narrows at top and can hold 5 ounce portion below midpoint

STEM

For swirling and maintaining temperature

NARROWER BASE FOR OLDER RED WINES

Pour gently or filter to separate wine from sediment and minimize aeration

WIDER BASE FOR YOUNGER WINES

Pour and swirl vigorously to maximize aeration

HOW TO CHOOSE A WINE GLASS

Wine glasses are never filled more than halfway. That's because wine glasses are designed for enhancing scent: their large bowls leave ample space above the surface of the wine so that the wine can be "swirled" without it spilling, and their long stems prevent our hands from warming the wine. Swirling increases the wine's surface area and, therefore, the evaporation rate of its aroma compounds, which are then trapped and concentrated in the headspace of the glass.

Wine glasses come in many sizes and shapes. Red wine glasses are often larger since red wines need more headspace than milder whites do. That said, a single multipurpose wine glass in the 12 to 14 ounce range can handle almost all wine needs: red and white, sparkling and dessert.

WHEN TO CONSIDER DECANTING WINE

In two circumstances, wines may benefit from being decanted into a clean serving vessel, but these only apply to premium age-worthy wines.

1. **To remove sediment in older red wines**

   Red wines release a fine sediment after ten or more years of aging in bottles (or sooner for unfiltered wines). Pouring the wine carefully into a decanter can separate the clear wine from these solids.

2. **To aerate and mellow younger wines**

   For wines that have yet to reach their peak, a little air can help flavors bloom and intensify, mimicking the flavor changes that would develop with longer cellaring.

Wine enhances any occasion. It is a noble elixir that needs special treatment and proper presentation to reveal its best."

Jeb

WHY SERVING TEMPERATURE MATTERS

Wine's flavor is extremely temperature-sensitive. Almost all wine styles are best served chilled—not just whites and sparkling wines but also rosés, dessert wines, and fortified wines—but serving wines ice-cold can make them taste bland. Try removing chilled wines from the refrigerator ten to fifteen minutes before serving to let them warm up a little. This will allow their flavors and scents to bloom.

Only red wines are not served chilled since the compounds that give them color can become harsh and bitter at low temperatures. Room temperature can be a little too warm, though, which can make reds seem boozy or lacking in refreshment. This can be easily remedied with ten to fifteen minutes in the refrigerator before pouring.

WHEN TO DRINK FINE WINES

Contrary to popular belief, most wines do not improve with age. It's true that many can be kept quite a while before they deteriorate, but their fresh fruit flavors will fade. Few wines are concentrated enough to develop new flavors and smells to replace the original flavors that are lost over time.

Any wines that will be drunk within a couple of months can be stored in the refrigerator or at room temperature, but long-term storage requires more wine-friendly conditions. The ideal conditions for wine storage are like those found in a natural basement: dark and damp, still and chilly. A temperature range of 50-60°F at roughly 60% humidity is ideal. Bottles sealed with natural cork should be laid on their sides.

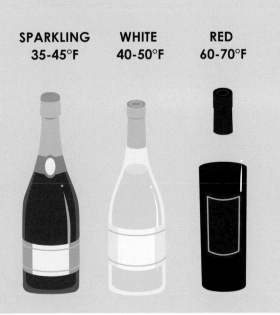

SPARKLING
35-45°F

WHITE
40-50°F

RED
60-70°F

OVER 90% OF WINES are designed to taste best immediately upon release.

FEWER THAN 10% are designed to taste better after aging 5 years after release.

FEWER THAN 1% are designed to taste better after aging 10 years or more after release.

DINING WITH WINE
DECIDING WHAT TO DRINK WHEN

Wine is an excellent food partner, like a special sauce on the side. There's no question that most foods taste better with wine than they do with other drinks. Unfortunately, few wine drinkers feel confident deciding which wine to serve with which foods. Since most meals combine all sorts of diverse foods, trying to match one perfect wine to the overall meal is usually more stressful than effective. For everyday meals, it's unnecessary to worry about pairing specific wines to specific dishes because simply aligning your wine with the time of year or time of day usually leads to great results. After all, seasonality affects what we're likely to be eating, anyway.

Sunshine—the same factor that has such a dramatic impact on wine flavor and style—has a strong influence on our wine cravings, too. We instinctively seek lighter, younger wines when the sun is up or when the weather is hot. Wines that deliver refreshment and can be served chilled fit the bill in the summer for the same reason we wear shorts and eat salads: they help us cool off. The reverse is true when the sun goes down or the temperature drops—that's when stronger, more complex wines make us feel warm and cozy. Essentially, lighter, cool-climate wines in the Vivacious and Elegant categories are better suited to help us beat the heat, while bold, strong, warm-climate wines like those in the Voluptuous and Powerful categories provide a little bottled sunshine that has the power to banish a wintry chill.

> "Wine adorns food like a beautiful jewel adorns a woman. . . . It is an essential element of any great meal that creates an incredible new dimension of flavor."
>
> *Jeb*

THE SUN AND OUR WINE CRAVINGS

When the sun is high or the weather is warm, we crave wines that are:	When the sun goes down or the weather is cool, we crave wines that are:
LIGHTER	HEAVIER
LOWER IN ALCOHOL	HIGHER IN ALCOHOL
PALER IN COLOR	DEEPER IN COLOR
MILDER IN FRUIT FLAVOR	BOLDER IN FRUIT FLAVOR
LOWER IN OAK FLAVOR	HIGHER IN OAK FLAVOR
MORE YOUTHFUL	MORE MATURE
MORE VIBRANT	MORE COMPLEX
SERVED COLDER	SERVED WARMER

TAKE YOUR PAIRINGS TO THE NEXT LEVEL

GOOD PAIRINGS

BETTER PAIRINGS

BEST PAIRINGS

SOMMELIER-STYLE REFINEMENTS

Advanced matching
to specific recipe

**ENTERTAINING
& DINING OUT**

Basic matching
to main ingredient

EVERYDAY OCCASIONS

Simple suitability
for the mood, season,
& time of day

Most wines taste great with most foods, so it's hard to go wrong when taking cues from the season, time of day, and degree of formality. When the occasion calls for something special, though, thinking like a sommelier can take your pairings from everyday to divine. Among professionals, the goal is to craft pairings where both the wine and food seem to magically taste better together than they did apart. Fortunately, you don't need encyclopedic wine knowledge to get there—you just need a few simple rules of thumb and a little insight into how our senses operate and how wine and food interact.

MATCHING WINE & FOOD
THE FLATTERING REWARDS OF PAIRING LIKE WITH LIKE

When choosing what to drink with dinner, most people have excellent natural instincts—more often than not, the simplest and most obvious strategy has the best results. The easiest way to find mutually flattering combinations (meaning that both the wine and the food taste better together than they would apart) is to "match" wines by choosing those wines that have a similar weight and flavor intensity to the food being served. Why? Because dining is a balancing act in which the food and wine compete for our attention. Sticking to wine that has a similar impact as the food levels the playing field. If a wine or a food feels richer or tastes stronger than its intended partner, it can detract from our appreciation. The goal is to achieve balance, where neither the food nor the wine overpowers the other.

MATCH WINES & FOODS OF SIMILAR WEIGHT

The most important trait to match is textural richness. We think of this as "weight." When we consider food options, we might want something that feels light (like a salad), or we might crave something heavier (like a steak). Regardless of portion size, what makes foods feel "lighter" or "heavier" is typically their fat content and protein density. In wine, perceived weight is controlled primarily by alcohol content, with the strongest wines feeling the heaviest on the palate. As a result, lightweight foods (like salads and shellfish) usually taste best with the lightest wines, while heavier foods (like cheeses and red meats) tend to pair best with heavier wines.

MATCH THE STRONGEST FLAVORS OF WINES AND FOODS

The next key factor to match is flavor intensity. Understated foods with mild flavors (like raw oysters or poached eggs) generally taste best with mild drinks, like sparkling wines or unoaked whites. Foods that taste inherently bolder (like lamb or blue cheese) tend to taste better with wines of similar aromatic amplitude, such as red wines and dessert wines.

> " The simplest path to harmony at the dinner table is to partner wines and foods that are similar in both weight and flavor concentration." *JeB*

However, it's important to remember to look beyond such proteins since so much of a dish's flavor is added during preparation. Most people instinctively pick their wines based solely on the main ingredient in what they're eating—a white for salmon, for instance, or a red for beef. When professionals pair wines, they usually focus less on which proteins are used and more on how the dish is made. That's because seasonings and cooking methods usually have a stronger flavor impact than the main ingredient alone. For example, a sommelier might pair the same white with a raw tartare (milder in flavor) or the same red with grilled steaks (bolder in flavor) regardless of whether these dishes are made using salmon or beef. The instinct to match is the same, but the matching is oriented around the strength and character of the most prominent flavors on the plate, rather than the main ingredients.

WHEN IN DOUBT, LIGHTEN UP

When you're not sure what will be served or if you're pairing for a diverse range of foods, err on the side of lighter, milder wines. Not only do they flatter lighter, milder foods, they can provide a pleasant counterpoint for more robust dishes, too. In general, the heavier the wine, the less flexible it is with food.

ADVANCED PAIRING INSIGHTS
SOMMELIER SECRETS OF WINE & FOOD CHEMISTRY

Wine and food are so good together that choosing wines by season or occasion is usually enough to achieve harmony. Matching wine to food's weight and flavor intensity works even better. However, it is possible to take your wine-pairing skills to the next level by learning a few tricks of the restaurant trade.

FORGET FISH OR MEAT! THINK SALTY OR SWEET

The levels of salt and sugar in a dish are often more important pairing factors than the main ingredients are:

- **Salt blocks the tongue's ability to discern acidity.** After a bite of salted food, high-acid wines usually taste softer and fruitier, which is why most of Europe's classic wines are so tart (French Burgundies, for example). These wines are designed to be a little too acidic on the first sip so they can taste their best alongside salty food. Less acidic wines, like California's more modern red blends, may taste great alone, but they don't fare as well when paired with high-salt foods—those foods make the wines seem heavier, clunkier, and less refreshing.

- **Sugar amplifies wine's perceived acidity and makes it taste less sweet and fruity.** Since wines are already quite acidic and most are not sweet, this effect is usually unpleasant. To avoid this problem, the wine served must be at least as sweet as the food. Foods with a touch of sweetness are far kinder to fruity modern wines than to drier traditional styles, but with overtly sugary sauces, the only safe choices are wines that are just as sweet.

SALTY OR SWEET?

SALT IN FOOD

LOWERS PERCEIVED ACIDITY IN WINE

INCREASES WINE'S PERCEIVED FRUITINESS

SUGAR IN FOOD

INCREASES PERCEIVED ACIDITY IN WINE

LOWERS WINE'S PERCEIVED FRUITINESS

> " Seasonings and sauces often trump other ingredients when it comes to pairing. Salt and fat are every dry wine's best friends, but sugar and spice can be their worst enemies."

JeB

> "Seasonings and sauces often trump other ingredients when it comes to pairing. Salt and fat are every dry wine's best friends, but sugar and spice can be their worst enemies."

JeB

"LIKE WITH LIKE" WORKS FOR EVERYTHING EXCEPT SPICY HEAT

Matching works as a strategy because our senses don't operate like bank accounts—most sensations don't "add up" to seem stronger together. Instead, similar sensations neutralize each other as our senses adjust in a way that is almost always harmonious. Whether the flavors in a dish are tangy or herbal, earthy or fruity, smoky or sweet, sommeliers will often choose wines that echo those dominant traits, regardless of the wine's color or whether the protein is meat or seafood. But there is one significant exception to this matching rule: it can backfire with spicy foods and "spicy" wines. Why? The same word is used for both, but it describes very different qualities. Spicy foods (like chili peppers) cause a physical burning sensation of heat. Wines described as "spicy" have aromatics that resemble spices (like those of pepper-scented Syrah) and are almost always strong wines with a higher alcohol content. Since alcohol acts as an irritant that makes the burn of spicy food seem more intense and painful—think of rubbing salt into a wound—sommeliers usually pair wines with the lowest possible alcohol content (like sparkling wines) with the spiciest foods. (Or they give up on wine and go with beer.)

WINE'S OAK LEVEL & FOOD'S COOKING METHOD

Whether roasted or grilled, baked or fried, foods that are browned during cooking acquire a layer of toasty, caramelized flavor that is not present in foods that are not browned.

These "toasty" flavors strongly resemble the flavors found in wines that are fermented or aged in oak barrels. Why? Wooden staves must be toasted over flames before they can be bent into rounded barrel shapes. As a result, foods that are raw or cooked without browning often pair best with younger, fresher-tasting wines that are not oak-aged. Foods that are browned in the cooking process usually make better partners for richer, more complex wines that have been aged or fermented in barrels.

DEGREES OF BROWNING

GRILLED	HEAVILY OAKED WINES
ROASTED	
BAKED	LIGHTLY OAKED WINES
POACHED	
RAW	UNOAKED WINES

CHOOSING WINES FOR VEGETABLES
PAIRING INSIGHTS FOR PLANT-BASED FOODS

Vegetables come in a veritable rainbow, and color-matching them with wines can produce terrific results. Corn shines with golden-hued white wines, like Chardonnay, while vivid beets work beautifully with violet-tinged young reds, like Beaujolais. Greens of all kinds adore leafy-tasting wines, like Sauvignon Blanc (even if these wines do smell greener than they look). Going past the basic vegetable color, our natural instinct to pair like with like is still right on the money—when sauces or seasonings provide stronger flavors than the veggies themselves do, match them accordingly and think of the wine as just another sauce on the side. Even when you're working with the same type of vegetable, how a dish is prepared makes a world of difference, as shown in the chart below, comparing suggestions by flavor profiles.

VEGETABLE PAIRING IDEAS BY WINE STYLE

The Spectrum of Style is a useful tool for choosing the right wine to serve with any type of food, and vegetables are no exception. Bright, tangy dressings and raw veggies call for bright, tangy young wines, while foods that have been roasted with butter to create an enriched texture or stewed with spices for deepened flavor are rewarded by heavier or more boldly flavored wines.

VIVACIOUS

Vivacious wines are ideal choices for most salads. Their bright, refreshing flavors make them ideal partners for veggies that are served raw or chilled, especially those with herbal flavors or high-acid dressings.

VOLUPTUOUS

Since they are plumper in texture and often feature a nutty hint of oak flavor, Voluptuous whites work best with the richer, creamier textures and bolder, toastier flavors of cooked foods.

	VIVACIOUS PAIRINGS	VOLUPTUOUS PAIRINGS
TOMATO	**Tomato Salad with Basil** JCB No. 69 Brut Rosé Crémant de Bourgogne	**Creamy Tomato Soup** LVE Chardonnay
BEANS	**Chilled Green Pea Soup** Raymond Sauvignon Blanc	**Garlicky Chickpea Hummus** Ropiteau Frères Puligny-Montrachet
GREENS	**Cucumber Salad with Dill** Jean-Claude Boisset Bourgogne Aligoté	**Wedge Salad with Blue Cheese** Buena Vista Carneros Chardonnay

WHAT NOT TO PAIR—COMMON CLASHES TO AVOID WITH VEGETABLES

Wine makes a terrific partner for most veggies, but not all wine and vegetable marriages are blissful. The most troublesome issue is that vegetables are quite low in components like fat, sodium, and protein, which can make it difficult for them to harmonize with the boldest red wines. Delicious pairings do exist for vegetarians, but the wines that work best skew strongly to the lighter, brighter end of the style spectrum. A few vegetables are often called "wine killers," but the dangers of these veggies are overhyped. It's true that both the slender asparagus and the portly artichoke contain compounds that can leave wines tasting strangely askew—most notably when these vegetables are barely cooked—but the right preparation can rectify the problem, such as cooking them with lemon or wine, butter or cheese.

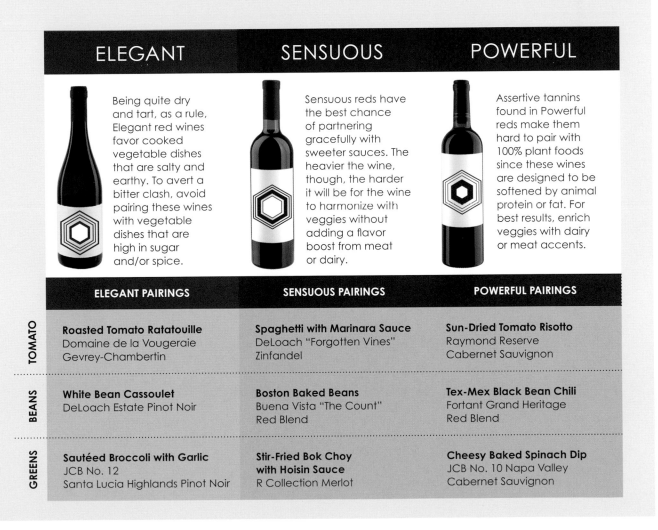

	ELEGANT	SENSUOUS	POWERFUL
	Being quite dry and tart, as a rule, Elegant red wines favor cooked vegetable dishes that are salty and earthy. To avert a bitter clash, avoid pairing these wines with vegetable dishes that are high in sugar and/or spice.	Sensuous reds have the best chance of partnering gracefully with sweeter sauces. The heavier the wine, though, the harder it will be for the wine to harmonize with veggies without adding a flavor boost from meat or dairy.	Assertive tannins found in Powerful reds make them hard to pair with 100% plant foods since these wines are designed to be softened by animal protein or fat. For best results, enrich veggies with dairy or meat accents.
	ELEGANT PAIRINGS	**SENSUOUS PAIRINGS**	**POWERFUL PAIRINGS**
TOMATO	**Roasted Tomato Ratatouille** Domaine de la Vougeraie Gevrey-Chambertin	**Spaghetti with Marinara Sauce** DeLoach "Forgotten Vines" Zinfandel	**Sun-Dried Tomato Risotto** Raymond Reserve Cabernet Sauvignon
BEANS	**White Bean Cassoulet** DeLoach Estate Pinot Noir	**Boston Baked Beans** Buena Vista "The Count" Red Blend	**Tex-Mex Black Bean Chili** Fortant Grand Heritage Red Blend
GREENS	**Sautéed Broccoli with Garlic** JCB No. 12 Santa Lucia Highlands Pinot Noir	**Stir-Fried Bok Choy with Hoisin Sauce** R Collection Merlot	**Cheesy Baked Spinach Dip** JCB No. 10 Napa Valley Cabernet Sauvignon

CHOOSING WINES FOR SEAFOOD
PAIRING INSIGHTS FOR THE OCEAN'S BOUNTY

There is a salty hint of the sea in virtually all fish, mollusks, and crustaceans that balances wine's natural acidity, creating a delightful tension. It's not a coincidence that most of our favorite seafood sauces are similarly tart, from tomato-based cocktail sauce to a simple squeeze of lemon. Most wine drinkers also instinctively choose wines that are light in color, light in flavor, or light in body (and sometimes all three) when deciding what to drink with what the French call *fruits de mer*, or the fruit of the sea. Raw or partly cooked seafood calls for understatement in a wine partner, but stronger-tasting cooking methods like smoking and grilling can merit more powerful wine flavors. Bold sauces and heaping helpings of spice do the same, as shown in the pairing examples sorted by wine style below.

SEAFOOD PAIRING IDEAS BY WINE STYLE

While there are seafood dishes that can pair reasonably well across the full Spectrum of Style, white, pink, and sparkling wines are their most successful partners. That said, as we move from the naked briny flavors of raw shellfish and sushi to cooked seafood dishes and fattier fish, our recipes get richer and more intense, and lighter, brighter red wines can sometimes be surprisingly flattering.

VIVACIOUS

It's hard to go wrong serving Vivacious wines with any type of seafood, but they are absolutely essential for dishes served raw and chilled and for those whose only seasoning is a bracing splash of lemon or vinegar.

VOLUPTUOUS

Being a little heavier and less tart, Voluptuous whites are natural choices when seafood has been smoked or browned during cooking or when seafood is served with richly textured sauces or caramelized accents.

	VIVACIOUS PAIRINGS	**VOLUPTUOUS PAIRINGS**
SHELLFISH	**Raw Oysters on the Half Shell** Buena Vista "La Victoire" Champagne	**New England Clam Chowder** Raymond Napa Valley Chardonnay
FISH	**Red Snapper Sashimi with Wasabi** J. Moreau & Fils Chablis	**Fried Haddock "Fish & Chips" with Tartar Sauce** Fortant "Hills Reserve" Viognier
OTHER SEAFOOD	**Fried Soft-Shell Crabs** JCB No. 5 Côtes de Provence Dry Rosé	**Steamed Lobster with Butter** Domaine de la Vougeraie Vougeot "Le Clos Blanc"

WHAT NOT TO PAIR—COMMON CLASHES TO AVOID WITH SEAFOOD

The "white wine with fish; red wine with meat" rule isn't hard and fast, but it does have a firm basis in food chemistry. Being naturally low in fat makes seafood light in both flavor and texture. As a result, the delicate character of fresh fish and shellfish can be easily overpowered by stronger accompaniments, whether those are sauces or wines. Since seafood rewards a light touch when it comes to seasonings, it's no surprise that milder-tasting wines like whites and rosés often have the pairing edge. Red wines can work nicely on occasion, but primarily with cooked seafood. The most flattering reds are lighter, paler, and younger, but for wine drinkers set on heavy hitters, consider boosting the intended dish into red wine terrain in terms of flavor and texture by cooking seafood with red wine or adding butter. Using cheese or even meat as a seasoning also helps.

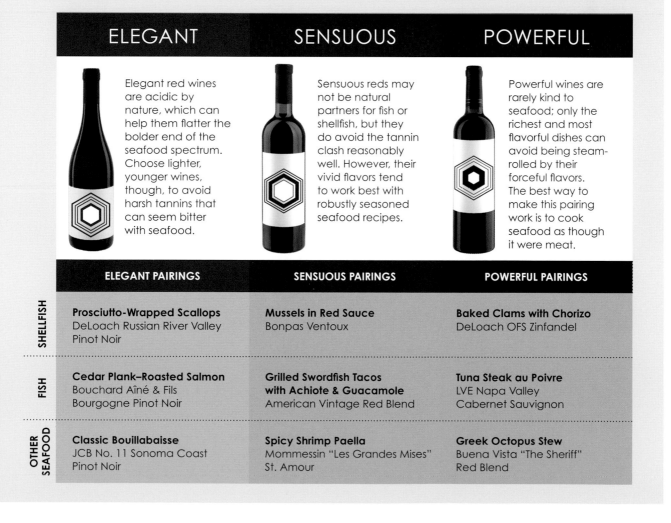

	ELEGANT	SENSUOUS	POWERFUL
	Elegant red wines are acidic by nature, which can help them flatter the bolder end of the seafood spectrum. Choose lighter, younger wines, though, to avoid harsh tannins that can seem bitter with seafood.	Sensuous reds may not be natural partners for fish or shellfish, but they do avoid the tannin clash reasonably well. However, their vivid flavors tend to work best with robustly seasoned seafood recipes.	Powerful wines are rarely kind to seafood; only the richest and most flavorful dishes can avoid being steam-rolled by their forceful flavors. The best way to make this pairing work is to cook seafood as though it were meat.
	ELEGANT PAIRINGS	**SENSUOUS PAIRINGS**	**POWERFUL PAIRINGS**
SHELLFISH	**Prosciutto-Wrapped Scallops** DeLoach Russian River Valley Pinot Noir	**Mussels in Red Sauce** Bonpas Ventoux	**Baked Clams with Chorizo** DeLoach OFS Zinfandel
FISH	**Cedar Plank–Roasted Salmon** Bouchard Aîné & Fils Bourgogne Pinot Noir	**Grilled Swordfish Tacos with Achiote & Guacamole** American Vintage Red Blend	**Tuna Steak au Poivre** LVE Napa Valley Cabernet Sauvignon
OTHER SEAFOOD	**Classic Bouillabaisse** JCB No. 11 Sonoma Coast Pinot Noir	**Spicy Shrimp Paella** Mommessin "Les Grandes Mises" St. Amour	**Greek Octopus Stew** Buena Vista "The Sheriff" Red Blend

CHOOSING WINES FOR MEATS
PAIRING INSIGHTS FOR MEATS & POULTRY

Meats are at the top of the food chain by virtue of containing very concentrated proteins, which translates to heaping helpings of flavor and texture. While the palest meats—think chicken and veal—may be considered white wine territory, darker meats (like beef and duck) generally favor the depth and heft found in red wines and rosés, so matching by flavor and matching by color often go hand in hand. Compared to other food groups, meats are not simply dense and flavorful—they're also naturally high in fat. Their tactile richness is one of the few components of food that's capable of softening the astringent tannic edge found in so many red wines. (Those tannins can leave the palate feeling leathery.) As a result, meats are the one category where red wines are as food-friendly as other wines. And since red wines are so wildly popular for their depth and complexity, this makes meats the most well-rounded of wine partners.

MEAT PAIRING IDEAS BY WINE STYLE

Since both vegetables and seafood tend to favor lighter, whiter wines, wine drinkers often see meats of all kinds as red wine's rightful territory. However, wide ranges of cooking methods and seasoning levels can yield meat dishes of every weight and intensity, so successful pairings can span the full Spectrum of Style.

VIVACIOUS

Except for their obvious synergy with cured meats, Vivacious wines are often overlooked, but their bracing tartness can offer a pleasing counterpoint to a much wider range of recipes.

VOLUPTUOUS

Among whites, Voluptuous wines are most often cheated of their right to partner with meats. They are sublime with white meats, of course, but also with red meats when the latter aren't over-seasoned.

	VIVACIOUS PAIRINGS	VOLUPTUOUS PAIRINGS
POULTRY	**Turkey with Cranberry Sauce** Fortant Grenache Rosé	**Rotisserie Chicken** DeLoach Estate Chardonnay
PORK	**BLT Sandwich** JCB No. 81 Sonoma Coast Chardonnay	**Pork Chops with Applesauce** Fortant "Coast Select" Muscat
BEEF	**Beef Carpaccio with Capers** JCB No. 21 Crémant de Bourgogne	**Chicken-Fried Steak** LVE Napa Valley Chardonnay

WHAT NOT TO PAIR—COMMON CLASHES TO AVOID WITH MEATS

Unlike vegetables and seafood, meats are so inherently wine-friendly that any clashes with wine are almost invariably due to mismatches in seasoning or cooking. Making assumptions about the kind of wine that must be served with meat probably does more to limit the average wine drinker's pleasure than anything else. For example, it is often assumed that only red wines have the ability to pair well with red meats, but anyone who has tried an exquisite Chardonnay or Champagne with their steak knows this to be nonsense. In short, the best way to avoid problems when pairing meat dishes with wines is to worry less about matching a wine to the type of protein and instead to navigate more by the flavor of the specific recipe (see chart below).

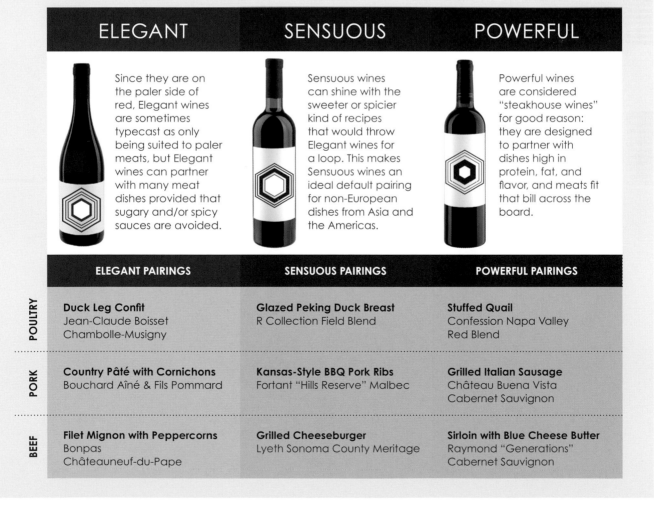

	ELEGANT	SENSUOUS	POWERFUL
	Since they are on the paler side of red, Elegant wines are sometimes typecast as only being suited to paler meats, but Elegant wines can partner with many meat dishes provided that sugary and/or spicy sauces are avoided.	Sensuous wines can shine with the sweeter or spicier kind of recipes that would throw Elegant wines for a loop. This makes Sensuous wines an ideal default pairing for non-European dishes from Asia and the Americas.	Powerful wines are considered "steakhouse wines" for good reason: they are designed to partner with dishes high in protein, fat, and flavor, and meats fit that bill across the board.
	ELEGANT PAIRINGS	**SENSUOUS PAIRINGS**	**POWERFUL PAIRINGS**
POULTRY	**Duck Leg Confit** Jean-Claude Boisset Chambolle-Musigny	**Glazed Peking Duck Breast** R Collection Field Blend	**Stuffed Quail** Confession Napa Valley Red Blend
PORK	**Country Pâté with Cornichons** Bouchard Aîné & Fils Pommard	**Kansas-Style BBQ Pork Ribs** Fortant "Hills Reserve" Malbec	**Grilled Italian Sausage** Château Buena Vista Cabernet Sauvignon
BEEF	**Filet Mignon with Peppercorns** Bonpas Châteauneuf-du-Pape	**Grilled Cheeseburger** Lyeth Sonoma County Meritage	**Sirloin with Blue Cheese Butter** Raymond "Generations" Cabernet Sauvignon

Buena Vista Winery & Vineyards
BOUCHARD AINE & FILS
DOMAINE DE LA VOUGERAIE
JCB
DLV

CHAPTER

THE MAGICAL WORLD OF BOISSET

VISITING FRENCH & AMERICAN WINE COUNTRY

A tour of Boisset's family collection of wineries in France and California encompasses some of the wine world's most spectacular destinations. From Burgundy's legendary Côte de Nuits to the romance of the Rhône, from California's first premium winery in Sonoma to the allure of Napa Valley, each Boisset winery offers its own unique and compelling environment in which to enjoy an unparalleled exploration of terroir, heritage, and vineyards with passion, emotion, and style.

JCB BY JEAN-CHARLES BOISSET
CELEBRATING TIME. TRANSCENDING TERROIR. EMBRACING STYLE.

Created by Jean-Charles Boisset, the innovative JCB Collection brings together two worlds of wine-making: the Old and the New. With the collection, Jean-Charles celebrates his French heritage while embracing his passion for California. Each wine in the collection is a limited edition and is "named" with a number. These numbers signify a wine style that Jean-Charles strives to achieve from vin-tage to vintage. At the same time, the numbers also symbolize important ideas, passions, and moments in his life and wine career.

EMBRACE THE WINE LIFE IN INIMITABLE STYLE

Set the tone for an unforgettable wine country journey with a luxe JCB experience at one of his sumptuous California locations. After a day of travel, you can make your way to an oasis of opulence and *joie de vivre*, whether you find yourself in San Francisco's JCB Lounge or Napa Valley's JCB Tasting Salon and Atelier Fine Foods. Surround yourself with the renowned Jean-Charles atmosphere of luxury, elegance, and sly whimsy while enjoying sumptuous settings that indulge the senses, inspire the creative spirit, and range from the surreal to the sublime.

BUENA VISTA WINERY
CALIFORNIA'S ORIGINAL PREMIUM WINERY

Before vineyards lined every valley north of San Francisco, before Napa and Sonoma were household names—before California was even on the wine world's map!—there was Buena Vista Winery. Founded in 1857, Buena Vista Winery is California's first premium winery, with a history that is as colorful as it is proud. Its founder, the legendary Count of Buena Vista, Agoston Haraszthy, is recognized as the "Father of California Wine" thanks to his introduction of fine wine grapes, his quality-minded innovations, and his early recognition of California's potential to become one of the world's top wine regions.

SET OUT TO EXPLORE
CALIFORNIA'S RICH WINE HISTORY

The natural place to begin any trip to California's wine country is with a visit to Buena Vista Winery. Discover where the story began with a tour of California's first wine caves, a historic wine tool museum, and a dramatic tasting room steeped in wine lore that's located in the state's first gravity flow winery.

DE LOACH VINEYARDS
PIONEER OF THE RUSSIAN RIVER VALLEY

Experience firsthand the cooling ocean breezes that make the Russian River Valley California's most prestigious cool-climate wine region for grapes like Pinot Noir and Chardonnay. Since 1975, DeLoach Vineyards has produced exceptional wines that spotlight the singular personality of of the Russian River Valley's terroir. Not only has DeLoach captured the region's character, they've also championed the practice of bottling small lots of single-vineyard wines. Picnic in the vineyards of this idyllic twenty-acre organic farm to fully enjoy the bounty of this certified Biodynamic estate. In the cellar, observe traditional Burgundian techniques (such as open-top wood fermenters and punch-downs by hand), which ensure ambitious, terroir-driven wines of distinction.

ENJOY A SUN-DRENCHED
SONOMA AFTERNOON OUTDOORS

There is no better vineyard for picnicking than this beautiful estate in the Russian River Valley's famed Olivet Bench, where you can sample wines of Burgundian finesse while surrounded by the estate's Biodynamic gardens and farm.

RAYMOND VINEYARDS
ICONIC LANDMARK OF THE NAPA VALLEY

One of Napa Valley's founding wineries, Raymond Vineyards celebrated its first harvest in 1974, thereby tracing its roots back to the beginnings of the region's fine wine–growing revolution. Today, Raymond ranks among the wine world's most dynamic wine destinations, dedicated to inspiring a passion for wine amidst an environment of creativity, elegance, and luxury. Best known for its signature Cabernet Sauvignon, Raymond also produces Merlot, Chardonnay, and Sauvignon Blanc from its estate vineyards and a network of local growers.

AN UNFORGETTABLE OASIS OF CREATIVITY

Visitors to Raymond will find delightful surprises around every corner as they experience the winery's progressive series of diverse settings that awaken curiosity and stimulate the senses, including the luxe Red Room, the spectacular Crystal Cellar, and even Napa Valley's first dog winery, where canine visitors can relax in the shady comfort of Frenchie Winery's dog beds made of wine barrels.

JEAN-CLAUDE BOISSET
THE ORIGIN OF A WINE FAMILY'S LEGACY

In 1961, then a tenacious eighteen-year-old, Jean-Claude Boisset founded his eponymous winery in Nuits-St.-Georges. Today, the winery is a prominent artisan Burgundy producer with an audacious, authentic style. The winemaker strives to create wines that evoke this legendary region's history and identity—traditions in which human intervention is discreetly kept to a bare minimum. Utilizing only native yeasts and never more than 30% new oak, the wines are concentrated, well-rounded, and naturally expressive of their diverse terroirs. The winery embraces the philosophy of the winemaker as a "vini-culturalist," someone who is equally engaged in the vineyard and in the cellar and builds close partnerships with growers to achieve the highest-quality wines.

FIND INNER PEACE AT THE CONVENT OF LES URSULINES

The tiny Burgundian hamlet of Nuits-St.-Georges is the world capital of Pinot Noir and is also where the family firm of Jean-Claude Boisset can be found—in the historic convent of Les Ursulines. From its walled garden of fruit trees and boxwoods to its labyrinthine cellars, the sense of serenity and intangible mystery at Les Ursulines is palpable. A stirring cathedral to wine and the history and terroir of Burgundy that was built atop the ancient cellars of the convent, today the winery is a monument to the region's singular significance to the wine world.

DOMAINE DE LA VOUGERAIE
PRESTIGE TERROIRS IN THE HEART OF BURGUNDY

Faithful to its origins in the Cistercian traditions that defined Burgundy, the Domaine de la Vougeraie is a family estate created by Jean-Charles and his sister, Nathalie, that unites a collection of the most prestigious and historical vineyards in Burgundy. It encompasses a patchwork of seventy-four plots covering forty-two hectares, two-thirds of which are on the Pinot Noir–centric Côte de Nuits and one-third of which are on the Chardonnay-driven Côte de Beaune. At the heart of it all is the legendary monopole of Vougeot Premier Cru, Le Clos Blanc de Vougeot. The winery strictly adheres to organic and Biodynamic farming practices in order to strike a balance between earth, plant, and humanity. The goal is to draw the best from the terroir through lovingly tended soils, and low yields, to obtain concentrated fruits with intense flavor. This hand-crafted style is an embodiment of elegance and the continual quest for a precise expression of terroir.

SAMPLE THE CRUS OF BURGUNDY IN THE HEART OF THE CÔTE D'OR
Situated on the quiet Rue de l'Église in Premeaux-Prissey, the winery at Domaine de la Vougeraie can host visitors for private tastings, strictly by appointment only.

BOUCHARD AÎNÉ & FILS
A HISTORIC TASTE OF BURGUNDIAN TRADITION

Founded in 1750 in Beaune (the town at the historic heart of the Burgundy region), Bouchard Aîné & Fils is one of the oldest wine companies in the region. For over two centuries, the winery has helped refine the reputation of Burgundy's Pinot Noir and Chardonnay wines by pursuing perfection in quality, authenticity in style, and prestige in name. Generations of *savoir faire* have resulted in mastery of grape selection, winemaking, and aging. The history of the first wine merchant families is rich and complex, yet few remain to champion their traditions. Bouchard Aîné & Fils is one of the few and is passionately proud of its history.

EXPLORE THE SENSES WITHIN THE WALLED CITY OF BEAUNE

The wine cellars of Bouchard Aîné & Fils are located in the Hôtel du Conseiller du Roy, built in 1743. This jewel of Burgundy architecture houses a one-of-a-kind experience for visitors that is known as the Tour of the Five Senses. The uncommon experience unveils wine's unique delights one sense at a time, leading up to a grand finale that incorporates a tasting of fine Burgundy wines.

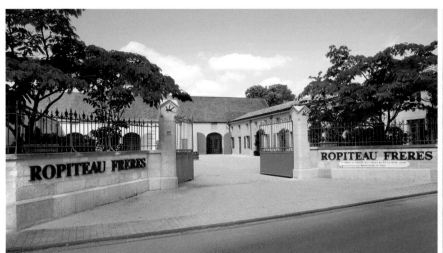

ROPITEAU FRÈRES
A CHAMPION OF CHARDONNAY

In 1848, the arrival of the railway in Burgundy spurred Jean Ropiteau to found a wine business with his brothers-in-law. In 1940, his great-grandson Auguste Ropiteau purchased the current cellars in Meursault and a property belonging to the Hospices de Beaune for a pittance. This acquisition became such a success that today the name Ropiteau Frères has become synonymous with the great wines of Burgundy's "golden triangle": the villages of Meursault, Puligny-Montrachet, and Chassagne-Montrachet. The majestic white wines of Ropiteau Frères embody the values of tradition, elegance, simplicity, and refinement.

STEP BACK IN TIME AT MEURSAULT'S CAVES DE L'HÔPITAL

The cellar of Ropiteau Frères was built in the seventeenth century and was formerly owned by the Hospices de Beaune. Under their stone arches, amidst the shadows and silence, the wines slowly ferment, just as they did over three centuries ago.

J. MOREAU & FILS
THE FINESSE OF A CHABLIS SPECIALIST

Since 1814, J. Moreau & Fils has built its reputation on a love of wine and a respect for the terroir that surrounds the remote village of Chablis, located in Burgundy's most remote northern district. J. Moreau & Fils has been rising to the challenge of farming this terroir—which is much cooler and cloudier than what the Côte d'Or experiences—with the sole aim of bringing out the very best of its single-grape variety, Chardonnay. The winery's white wines are complex, elegant, and balanced with precision. Their signature minerality and lively acidity levels craft a perfect equilibrium between terroir, fruit, structure, and texture, making the wines accessible in their youth, while they simultaneously possess a great aging potential.

FEEL THE CHALLENGES OF CLIMATE AND TERROIR IN CHABLIS

In Chablis, a short and chilly growing season pushes the Chardonnay grape to extremes, a process that coaxes out some of the most noble and expressive wines in the region. This is particularly evident in the wines grown in the appellation's *Premier Cru* and *Grand Cru* vineyards, where uncommonly pale soils and fossilized marine sediments help ripen grapes with their reflected sunlight.

CHÂTEAU DE PIERREUX
A BREATHTAKING BEAUJOLAIS ESTATE

A 250-acre estate facing the famed Mont Brouilly, Château de Pierreux is one of the region's treasures. Steeped in several centuries of history, the Château embodies the spirit of the Beaujolais region at its noblest. Almost 200 acres of Gamay vines (along with some plots of Pinot Noir) are farmed according to Biodynamic principles, allowing the Château to offer its most expressive wines. The complete origins of the property are lost to the mists of time, but the fortified towers that frame the manor date to the thirteenth century, and the wine cellars were excavated in the 1600s. Two wines—the Brouilly Château de Pierreux and the Réserve du Château de Pierreux—reveal the best of *Cru Beaujolais* winemaking.

MOMMESSIN
WHERE BURGUNDY MEETS BEAUJOLAIS

Mommessin has been bringing together the two neighboring wine cultures of Beaujolais and Burgundy since its founding in 1865. Its excellent wines are sourced from growers with long-term contracts, some of which are over one hundred years old and each of which is emblazoned with the iconic Mommessin seal. In 1889, Mommessin acquired several ancient stone buildings in Mâcon that originally belonged to the legendary Benedictine Abbey of Cluny. The abbey's emblem—the Key of Saint Peter—became an enduring symbol for all Mommessin wines and continues to grace their labels to this day. Mommessin is leading a revolution in the Beaujolais region: restoring the region's reputation for high-quality *Cru Beaujolais* wines crafted using Burgundian techniques,

BONPAS
AN ANCIENT LANDMARK OF THE RHÔNE VALLEY

Located within the boundaries of Châteauneuf-du-Pape (France's first controlled appellation of origin), the fortified convent at Bonpas has watched over the historic route that once linked Rome with Avignon since 1318. A visit to this gateway to the southern Côtes-du-Rhône allows you to discover the terroirs of the Rhône Valley through their distinctive wines. In this region, pale, smooth, round stones absorb the rays of the sun during the day and warm the vines at night, an effect that yields wines of power, nobility, and grace. This region is known for its abundance of grape varieties, each of which brings its own personality to a blend, from the leading star grape, Grenache, to fiery Syrah to moody Mourvèdre and beyond.

EXPERIENCE THE CHAPEL AT THE CHARTREUSE DE BONPAS

Visitors to this magnificent historic site can tour the twelfth century chapel, the French-style gardens, and the main courtyard. An array of Rhône wines are on offer in the Oenothèque de Bonpas; private tastings of these Rhône Valley wines also can be arranged in the ancient wine cellar.

FORTANT
A NEW VISION
OF THE LANGUEDOC

The Languedoc on France's Mediterranean coast lies at a crossroads of civilizations and climates, where a diversity of landscapes creates a wide range of wines shaped by both nature and man. Launched in 1988, Fortant de France created the first range of varietal wines in France, a change that simplified wine labeling for modern wine lovers and revolutionized one of the most ancient and most vast wine-growing regions in the world. Today, Fortant continues to pioneer innovative new ways of thinking with its three families of wines: Mountains Grand Reserve, Hills Reserve, and Coast Select.

SAVOR THE SOUTH OF FRANCE DOWN BY THE SEA

Breathe in the inspiration of the Mediterranean at Fortant, located in the picturesque seaside resort of Sète, known as the Venice of the Languedoc. Sample the exceptional array of fine wines that can be produced in one of the world's largest and most diverse wine regions.

FRANCE
& THE USA

WINE LABELS & WINE REGIONS

Once we understand how grape flavors shift with ripeness and why geography and culture affect how wines taste, wine labels that used to be confusing become easier to read. Studying the maps of major wine regions becomes much more productive, too. This helpful reference section explains how to read French and American wine labels and also summarizes the most salient details of key wine regions like California, Burgundy, and the south of France.

READING AMERICAN WINE LABELS
THE MODERN "VARIETAL" FORMAT

In New World regions like California, most wines are marketed under what is known as a "varietal label." This modern approach to wine labeling prominently lists the wine's main grape variety as an indicator of the wine's flavor or style.

Regardless of the origin of the grapes, all wine labels must list their vintner or brand identity along with their "appellation," which is a regulated statement of the fruit's region of origin. Every country also has its own requirements for the fine print on back labels. For fine wines, it is common for labels to also name the vintage year, but this is not required.

WHAT'S ON THE LABEL?

1 WINE APPELLATION
MANDATORY—A formal region-of-origin statement is required for all wines, which indicates where the grapes were grown (note that this is not necessarily where the wine was made). In many countries, including the U.S., political districts like states and counties automatically qualify as wine appellations. However, American fine wines more often come from smaller wine-specific appellations known as American Viticultural Areas or AVAs, as with Carneros, shown here.

2 BRAND NAME
MANDATORY—Wines are most often sold under the name of a winery, as shown here, but may also appear under a proprietary name or brand name (see item 9).

3 GRAPE VARIETY
OPTIONAL—Wines are typically labeled by the type of grape used, in which case they must contain at least 75% of the named variety.

4 VINTAGE DATE
OPTIONAL—This identifies the year in which the grapes were harvested.

5 FINE PRINT
MANDATORY—Legal requirements vary by country, but all wine bottles must indicate, on the front or back label: bottle volume, alcohol content, and country of origin. The company or facility that made the wine and its location must also be formally identified.

Many other types of information may also be listed on labels, some regulated and meaningful and some less so. Vintners often make more than one wine from the same grape and region—a basic version and a premium version, for example. To distinguish these from one another, they are given what is known in the trade as "*cuvée* names" (from the French term for "vat" or "batch"), which provide labels with additional specificity.

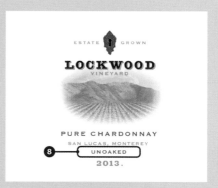

6 QUALITY INDICATORS
These may include informal designations of superiority, such as "Reserve," or regulated statements, like "Estate-Bottled."

7 SINGLE-VINEYARD DESIGNATIONS
Naming the site where the grapes were grown is another way of signaling that a wine has higher quality potential and is subject to stricter quality standards.

8 STYLE REFERENCES
Includes a range of terms that provide hints about flavor or style, such as "Sparkling," "Brut," "Unoaked," "Rosé," or "Late Harvest."

9 BRANDING IDENTIFIERS
Winery-specific names can distinguish amongst any given winery's offerings: single-wine "proprietary names" (A), multi-wine "series names" (B), and semi-independent "brand names" (C).

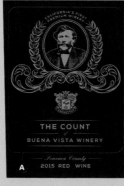

READING FRENCH WINE LABELS
THE TRADITIONAL "REGIONAL" FORMAT

Top French wines are not traditionally named for their grapes—they're named according to their region of origin or "appellation," such as Chablis or Côtes du Rhône. Following the French model, the European Union regulates wine label statements in its own way, one that links wine quality to regional specificity. Elsewhere, wine appellations simply certify where a wine's fruit was grown. In Europe, vintners must conform to far more stringent regulations in order to earn the right to use place names on labels. Regional appellations are the organizing principle behind wide-ranging quality standards in everything from grape growing to winemaking; appellations also serve as their own enforcement mechanism by formalizing local traditions into law. Appellations might mandate only using native grape varieties, and most limit crop size per vine by regulating the maximum yield per hectare.

French appellations are almost always place names: Bordeaux is a bustling port city, while Beaune is a walled town in the heart of Burgundy; Champagne and Côtes-du-Rhône are large regions, while Chablis and Beaujolais are smaller districts. In France, a wine's distinguishing feature and point of pride is its region of origin, not its grape. For example, the Meursault shown below is from a village of the same name. By law, the wine is made entirely with Chardonnay, but in keeping with French tradition, its label makes no reference to grape variety. This pattern dominates among the most traditional and ambitious of wines, but globalization is leading many vintners to mention the grape variety on the label, especially for value wines and those intended for international markets.

French appellations are often organized in hierarchies, with smaller, premium appellations carving out the best sites within larger, less prestigious ones (as shown on the opposite page). This arcane system developed over centuries in the Burgundy region, where wines from superior vineyard sites—known as *crus*—have long been bottled separately and accorded an elite status. Nowadays, "cru" status is encoded in Burgundy's legal appellation structure. Confusingly, Champagne, Bordeaux, and Alsace have also adopted the cru concept, but each regulates its use differently.

FRENCH WINE APPELLATION
The regulated place name, or appellation, is always in large text. Adjacent smaller text specifies the legal category, which in this case is the premium level *Appellation d'Origine Contrôllée,* or AOC.

BURGUNDY'S REGIONAL HIERARCHY OF WINE LABELING

These six labels are all for red wines made with 100% Pinot Noir from the Burgundy region, but their legal appellations specify smaller and smaller regions of origin. In the European system, greater specificity means stricter quality standards, more distinctive flavor, and more limited supply, all of which usually results in higher prices.

REGIONAL APPELLATIONS

Wines labeled "Bourgogne"—the French word for Burgundy—can be made from fruit grown anywhere within the region's legal boundaries unless a subdistrict is named in the appellation (as shown at far right).

A Regional Appellation
(strict quality standards)

B Subdistrict Appellation
(stricter quality standards)

C Grape Variety (optional)

D Cuvée Name (optional)

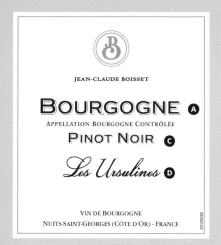

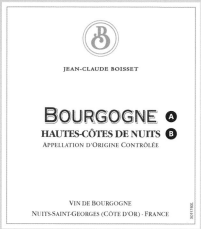

VILLAGE APPELLATIONS

Within Burgundy, some municipalities are granted their own appellation status since they make superior wines of distinctive character. Both labels here indicate "village-level" red wines from the village of Chambolle-Musigny. The one on the right also names its vineyard site, or *lieu dit*, which implies higher quality.

A Village Appellation
(much stricter quality standards)

B Unranked Single Vineyard
(implies higher quality)

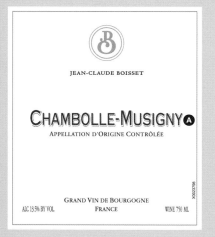

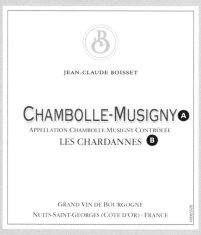

VINEYARD APPELLATIONS

Over the centuries, more than 400 individual vineyard sites in Burgundy have made such superb wines that they have earned their own appellations. The top 33 have *Grand Cru* status, where only their vineyard is named (as with the label at far right). The rest are next-best *Premier Crus*, where both the village and vineyard are named, in the formal appellation (as with the label at near right).

A *Premier Cru* Single Vineyard Appellation
(even stricter quality standards)

B *Grand Cru* Single Vineyard Appellation
(exceptionally strict quality standards)

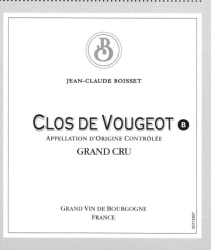

BURGUNDY

Burgundy—the English name of the Bourgogne region of France—takes its name from the medieval Duchy of Burgundy, whose seat of power was in the city of Dijon. Burgundy's boundaries have shifted considerably over the centuries, but in the twentieth century, Bourgogne was established as a political region of France, which comprised all of the historical wine regions of Burgundy. In 2014, Bourgogne was merged with a neighboring region to form Bourgogne-Franche-Comté. Within this region today, three French *départements* are home to the wine districts of Burgundy. Chablis is in the Yonne *département* to the north, and the Mâconnais and Côte Chalonnaise are located in the Sâone et Loire *département* to the south. In between the two, the vineyards of the so-called "golden slope" of Burgundy were of such renown that the zone's moniker was given to the *département*: the Côte d'Or.

THE ORIGINAL HIERARCHY OF APPELLATIONS

The core principle of wine appellations is to reward superior wine regions by granting them exclusive rights to use a respected place name in the same way that Florida oranges are marketed on the strength of that region's reputation for quality. Wine appellations take this concept considerably further by recognizing multiple layers of smaller and smaller and better and better subregions. This system was pioneered by the Cistercian monks of medieval Burgundy, who were the first to use terms like *terroir* and *cru* to recognize the difference in quality potential between one vineyard and another.

Since it takes time for the best appellations to earn recognition, the oldest wine regions, like Burgundy, will always have the most complicated appellation structure. Whole books have been written on the appellations of Burgundy; the region's famously fractionalized terrain and arcane wine laws are too complex to explain fully here. However, the fundamentals are as follows.

Any wine whose grapes were grown anywhere in the official Burgundy region is entitled to the Bourgogne appellation, provided that the wine meets stringent minimum quality standards. However, the Bourgogne region also encompasses over one hundred other smaller appellations. In areas of modest quality potential, wines may only be entitled to the basic regional Bourgogne appellation or to a smaller district appellation, like Chablis or Mâcon. In prime locations, though, appellations can nest many layers deep, from region to district to village to an individual vineyard site.

Single-vineyard appellations denote the very best Burgundy wines—only a few dozen of these so-called *Grand Crus* are recognized, with some being no larger than a football field. The highest quality standards are mandated for these smallest appellations.

GEOGRAPHY & CLIMATE

Since Burgundy lies on the cold end of the climate spectrum, its vineyards perform best when planted in warmer sites that are sheltered from incoming winds and storms. Some of the very finest wines of Burgundy come from hillside vineyards that have southern or southeastern exposure, where they get maximum benefits from the warming rays of the sun and shelter from storms and prevailing winds. In a few select places where such terrain coincides with a particularly suitable soil type, the resulting wines are so far superior to those of neighboring sites that they are recognized as *Grand Cru* vineyards (these are found only in the Côte d'Or and Chablis districts).

BURGUNDY'S FOUR MAIN WINEMAKING ZONES

CHABLIS	This is Burgundy's coldest region, located closer to the vineyards of Champagne than to Burgundy's other districts. Chablis produces only white wines, most with little or no oak influence. These wines tend to be lighter and leaner than other white Burgundies.
CÔTE D'OR	All of Burgundy's very best vineyards are in this tiny strip of land (see page 169). The finest reds come from the northern half, known as the Côte de Nuits; the finest whites come from the southern half, called the Côte de Beaune. These wines serve as the archetypes for international Pinot Noir and Chardonnay wines.
CÔTE CHALONNAISE	Villages in this small district, like Mercurey and Rully, have less prestige than those within the Côte d'Or, but they are known for their well-made and affordable white and red wines.
MÂCONNAIS	This large district is best known for its value-priced white Burgundies from appellations like Mâcon and Mâcon-Villages, but a handful of premium villages, such as Pouilly-Fuissé and St. Véran, have more quality potential and, therefore, greater prestige.

BURGUNDY'S CÔTE D'OR

Burgundy's finest wines are grown along an escarpment known as the Côte d'Or, where a geological upthrust of land creates a long, southeast-facing slope. The Côte d'Or stretches roughly thirty miles to the south and west from Dijon. Historically, the two main towns were called Beaune and Nuits; the larger Côte d'Or is still often subdivided into the Côte de Nuits to the north and the Côte de Beaune to the south.

These vineyards have been cultivated for so many centuries that their strengths and weaknesses have been well documented. The combination of soils and terrain in the Côte de Nuits is ideal for Pinot Noir, and since this is the region's most respected grape, little else is planted here. Fans of great red Burgundies soon discover that the wines from this area are denser, meatier, and longer-lived than any others the region can offer, which helps explain why a staggering percentage of Côte de Nuits wines are entitled to superior *Grand Cru* and *Premier Cru* appellations.

Farther south, the Côte de Beaune is more varied in terrain and less dominated by Pinot Noir or by single-vineyard appellations. Most of the red wines here are lighter and more elegant (with the exception of forceful Pommard) and are often seen as wines to be enjoyed young. When it comes to Chardonnay, however, the Côte de Beaune is unrivaled in producing Burgundy's finest white wines from two clusters of *Grand Cru* sites: those centered on Corton-Charlemagne in the north and those surrounding Le Montrachet in the south.

A CASE STUDY IN TERROIR—DISSECTING THE CÔTE DE NUITS

Topography is not the only significant factor of terroir, but in the Côte de Nuits escarpment, the vineyards located midslope tend to make the best wines. Many of these sites have been rewarded with *Grand Cru* status. Grapes grown just above or below perform almost as well, so these vineyards are classified as either next-best *Premier Cru* sites or as more modest village wines bottled under the name of their municipality. Marginal sites at the top and bottom of the slope produce lesser wines that are bottled either with less-prestigious district appellations, like Hautes Côtes de Nuits, or as a generic regional Bourgogne.

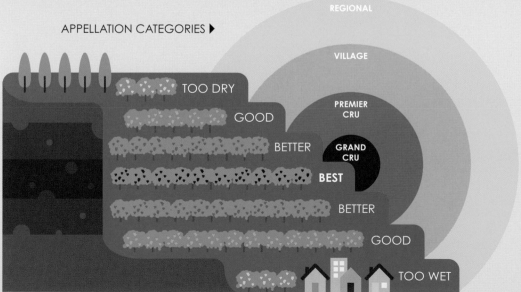

APPELLATION CATEGORIES ▶

REGIONAL

VILLAGE

PREMIER CRU

GRAND CRU

TOO DRY

GOOD

BETTER

BEST

BETTER

GOOD

TOO WET

THE SLOPES OF NUITS & BEAUNE

The Côte de Nuits is the smaller of the two subzones of the Côte d'Or. It produces almost exclusively Pinot Noir and is home to a stunning twenty-four *Grand Cru* vineyards in legendary villages like Vougeot, Vosne-Romanée, Chambolle-Musigny, and Gevrey-Chambertin.

The Côte de Beaune is a larger area, where the Côte d'Or escarpment breaks up into smaller hills. It produces both white and red wines in famed villages like Meursault, Puligny-Montrachet, Chassagne-Montrachet, Volnay, Aloxe-Corton, and Pommard. Of its eight *Grand Cru* vineyards, all but one—Le Corton—are white-only appellations.

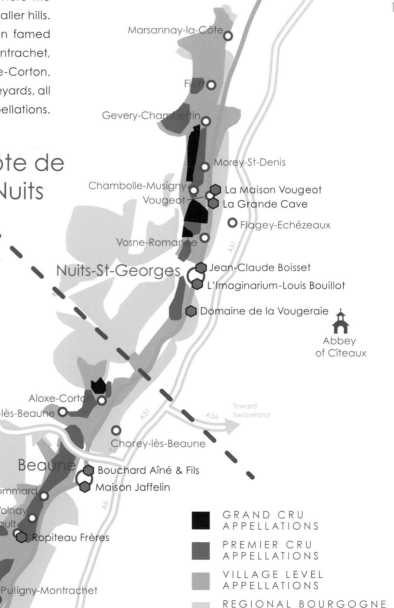

GRAND CRU
APPELLATIONS

PREMIER CRU
APPELLATIONS

VILLAGE LEVEL
APPELLATIONS

REGIONAL BOURGOGNE
APPELLATION

VILLAGE OR TOWN WITH
APPELLATION STATUS

BOISSET COLLECTION
WINERIES

THE SOUTH OF FRANCE

The South of France has a sun-drenched climate that both people and vines find quite accommodating. Historically, the finest wines came from colder regions, such as Burgundy, Champagne, and Bordeaux, while different vines produced larger amounts of lesser wines in warmer places. But today, truly spectacular wines can be made in warmer regions as well, such as the Beaujolais region, the Rhône Valley, Provence, and the Languedoc.

Traveling south from Burgundy, the climate begins to warm as we travel through the Beaujolais region and approach France's gastronomic capital of Lyon. Continuing farther south through the Rhône Valley, oak forests give way to orchards as the climate becomes more overtly Mediterranean. Once we reach the sea, whether we turn west toward the Languedoc or east into Provence, we are surrounded by olive groves and the distinctively aromatic scrubland of lavender, rosemary, and thyme called *la garrigue*.

THE FOUR MAIN WINEMAKING ZONES OF THE SOUTH OF FRANCE

BEAUJOLAIS	The Beaujolais region lies just south of Burgundy's Mâconnais district. Being slightly warmer with markedly different soils, this region does not suit Pinot Noir, so its vineyards are instead planted with one of its descendants: the red Gamay grape. Gamay is best known for its sappy, lightweight "Nouveau" wines, but when made with Burgundian methods in the region's so-called "Cru Villages," it can make age-worthy wines that are delicate yet complex.
RHÔNE VALLEY	The Rhône Valley wine region is considerably warmer than the Beaujolais region, but it also grows mostly red grapes. Its wines are stronger, spicier, and often blended, made with more robust grape varieties, like Grenache and Syrah. The region's most famous wines hail from the southern Rhône. Côtes-du-Rhône is the basic regional appellation here, but superior wines can be found in smaller village appellations, like Châteauneuf-du-Pape and Gigondas.
PROVENCE	While both red and white wines are made in Provence, this region is famous worldwide for its distinctively pale and dry rosé wines, typically made with the grapes of the Rhône, such as Grenache and Cinsault. This style gained popularity here partly because the climate favors robust red grapes, but lighter, chilled wines partner best with the region's cuisine, which centers on seafood, fresh produce, and olive oil.
LANGUEDOC-ROUSSILLON	The Languedoc and Roussillon regions are among the oldest wine regions in France, but in the modern era, they have been known for producing large quantities of everyday wines, rather than focusing on quality. In recent decades, however, both regions have made significant improvements and have earned recognition for their red wines in particular. The Rhône grapes Grenache and Syrah are widely planted here, but Carignane grapes (of Spanish origin) are more traditional and provide soulful wines from older vineyards. The Languedoc region was among the first in France to adopt American-style labeling by grape; its approach to warm-climate winemaking creatively blends French-style tradition with American-style innovation.

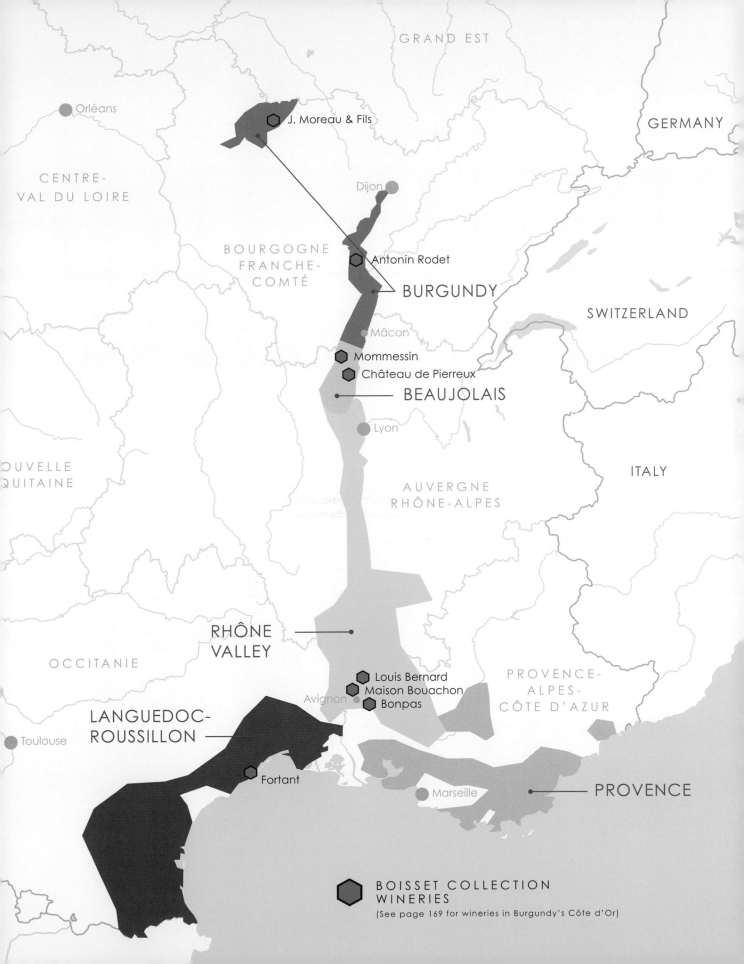

GRAND EST

Orléans

GERMANY

CENTRE-
VAL DU LOIRE

J. Moreau & Fils

Dijon

BOURGOGNE
FRANCHE-
COMTÉ

Antonin Rodet

BURGUNDY

SWITZERLAND

Mâcon

NOUVELLE
AQUITAINE

Mommessin

Château de Pierreux

BEAUJOLAIS

Lyon

ITALY

AUVERGNE
RHÔNE-ALPES

OCCITANIE

RHÔNE
VALLEY

PROVENCE-
ALPES-
CÔTE D'AZUR

Louis Bernard

Maison Bouachon

LANGUEDOC-
ROUSSILLON

Avignon

Bonpas

Toulouse

Fortant

Marseille

PROVENCE

BOISSET COLLECTION
WINERIES

(See page 169 for wineries in Burgundy's Côte d'Or)

CALIFORNIA

Nearly 90% of American wine is made in California. If the Golden State were its own nation, it would rank as the world's fourth-largest wine producer, behind only France, Italy, and Spain. Wines from California have shown promise since the late 1800s, but major setbacks derailed their progress for a hundred years. That said, California vintners and American wine drinkers are now leading forces in the global wine boom, which began in the 1970s and went on to revolutionize the wine world. Today, California makes some of the finest wines on earth. Only 15% of its wines are exported to other countries.

GEOGRAPHY & CLIMATE

Since California is very large in area—roughly two-thirds the size of France!—it can be difficult to make sweeping generalizations about its climate and geography. There are regions within the state where it is too hot to grow grapes but also regions where it is too cold for them to ripen. Broadly speaking, though, most of California's wine regions are sunnier and warmer and get less rainfall than the growing regions of France. As a result, California grapes typically reach higher degrees of ripeness and are known for making stronger, fruitier, and more richly textured wines.

The broad and fertile Central Valley is the state's agricultural heart and produces most of its bulk wine. However, this inland region is simply too hot for fine-wine growing, so California's premium wine zones all hug the Pacific, where fruit's rush to ripeness is slowed by cooling ocean breezes and coastal fog. California's finest wines hail from what are known as the Coastal Ranges, which are the hills and smaller valleys that stretch north and south from San Francisco Bay. Latitude has little effect on a vineyard's climate in these areas; instead, the climate is entirely dependent on how far a given vineyard is from the ocean and its relation to the mountains that surround and shelter it.

GEOGRAPHY OF A VINE-FRIENDLY CLIMATE

The reason for the vine-friendly climate of California's North Coast and Central Coast regions becomes clear when we study the relevant geography. Ocean currents force cold water to the surface along this stretch of coastline; in the meantime, when temperatures rise in the large flat basin of the Central Valley, the hot air there rises. This creates a suction effect that draws colder air and fog inland from the coast through the valleys and gaps in the coastal hills.

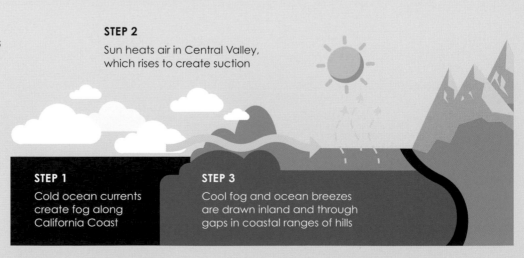

STEP 2

Sun heats air in Central Valley, which rises to create suction

STEP 1

Cold ocean currents create fog along California Coast

STEP 3

Cool fog and ocean breezes are drawn inland and through gaps in coastal ranges of hills

AMERICAN WINE APPELLATIONS, OR AVAS

Legally designated wine appellations in the United States are called American Viticultural Areas, or AVAs. Political regions like counties and states are de facto wine appellations under American law as well, but AVAs define regions whose wines share distinctive traits based on geography and climate. These can be huge multi-county areas, like California's Central Coast, or tiny ones, like Napa Valley's Stag's Leap District.

All American wines must list their appellations on the front label, but these are regulated more loosely in the New World than they are in Europe. As a result, American wine appellations do not mandate which grapes may or may not be grown, nor do they impose minimum quality standards or carve out complex nested hierarchies down to the vineyard level. Unlike European appellations, where 100% of the grapes must always be sourced from within the named region's boundaries, the American system has more wiggle room, requiring only a 75% minimum for state or county wines or an 85% minimum for AVA wines.

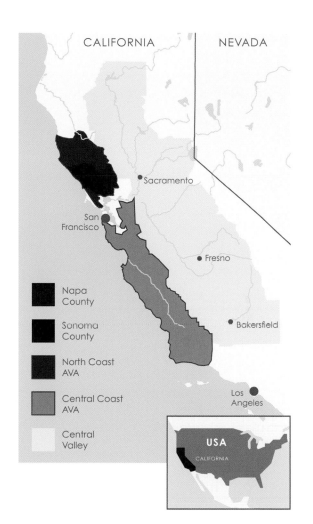

CALIFORNIA'S THREE MAIN WINEMAKING ZONES

NORTH COAST AVA	This is the heart of California wine country, where the most famous and historic wine regions of the North Coast sprawl across four counties: Napa, Sonoma, Mendocino, and Lake. Top AVAs include: Napa Valley, Russian River Valley, Sonoma Coast, Sonoma Valley, Rutherford, Carneros, St. Helena, Dry Creek Valley, Stag's Leap District, Oakville, Alexander Valley, Calistoga
CENTRAL COAST AVA	This larger, more recently developed wine region has great potential and encompasses key counties like Monterey, Santa Barbara, Santa Cruz, and San Luis Obispo. Top AVAs include: Santa Lucia Highlands, Paso Robles, Santa Ynez Valley, Edna Valley, Santa Maria Valley
CENTRAL VALLEY	While not an AVA, this flat and fertile region produces most of California's bulk and value-priced wines. Some subdistricts with higher quality potential, like Lodi and Clarksburg, have their own AVAs.

SONOMA COUNTY

Sonoma County is located an easy drive away from San Francisco, across the Golden Gate Bridge and just north of the scenic suburbs and redwood forests of Marin County. The earliest successes in California's winemaking history took place here in the nineteenth century, not long after the Bear Flag of the California Republic was first raised over the town of Sonoma itself. Sonoma County is one of the twin anchors of California wine country, along with its eastern neighbor, Napa Valley. Sonoma's terrain is well-suited to agriculture; today, this area is not only renowned for being a source of great wines but is also a leader in the farm-to-table movement that is home to great beers and great cheeses.

GEOGRAPHY & CLIMATE

Sonoma is the largest county within the North Coast AVA and features the most variation in climate. Temperatures here largely depend on proximity to the coast. Cool air off the water is able to penetrate the coastal hills at three points: the Russian River Valley, the Petaluma Gap, and the San Pablo Bay. This maritime influence cools the vineyards in Sonoma's westernmost and southernmost reaches, where vintners naturally specialize in cool-climate wine styles, like Chardonnay, Pinot Noir, and sparkling wines. Sonoma's more sheltered inland appellations are located to the north and east, along the Mayacamas range of mountains that separate Sonoma from Napa Valley. Being warmer and drier, these regions are better-suited for making heavier reds, such as Zinfandel and Cabernet Sauvignon.

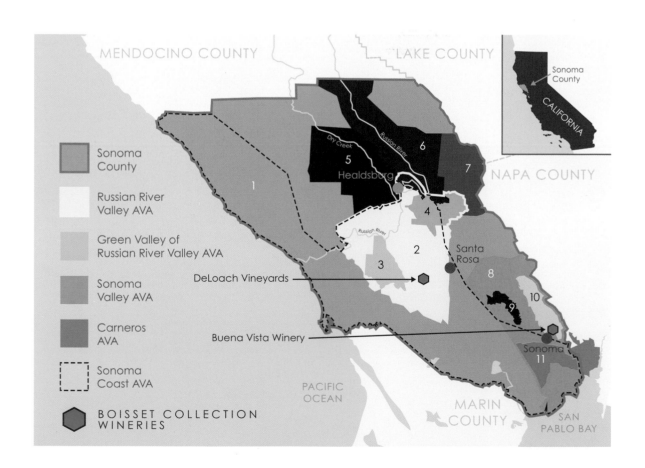

SONOMA'S OVERLAPPING WEB OF AVAS

There are sixteen AVAs in Sonoma County, but some are either so small or so new that they are not of much significance. The region's eleven main AVAs are listed below. Most are well-defined subregions with fairly consistent climate traits, like Russian River Valley and Dry Creek Valley. Unlike Napa Valley, many of Sonoma's AVAs overlap, most notably the large Sonoma Coast AVA. In some cases, an AVA may feature a subregion with its own AVA, as with the AVA earned by the Green Valley of Russian River Valley.

SONOMA COUNTY'S MAIN WINEMAKING ZONES

1 **SONOMA COAST AVA**	This massive wine region's boundaries were drawn to encompass the areas of Sonoma County most impacted by the cooling effects of the Pacific and the Bay. Best known for premium Chardonnay and Pinot Noir.
2 **RUSSIAN RIVER VALLEY AVA** 3 **GREEN VALLEY OF RUSSIAN RIVER VALLEY AVA** 4 **CHALK HILL AVA**	The winding Russian River allows cooling ocean breezes and daily summer fogs to penetrate deep inland. The Russian River Valley AVA is one of the most prestigious in the U.S. for Chardonnay and Pinot Noir. The Green Valley, best known for its sparkling wines, is the coolest subregion of the Russian River Valley and is entitled to its own appellation. The Chalk Hill AVA is the Russian River Valley's warmest subdistrict, where some heavier reds can ripen better.
5 **DRY CREEK VALLEY AVA** 6 **ALEXANDER VALLEY AVA** 7 **KNIGHTS VALLEY AVA**	These warmer areas of Sonoma, stretching north and west from Sonoma's winemaking hub of Healdsburg, are sheltered from ocean breezes and grow mostly red grapes such as Cabernet Sauvignon, Zinfandel, Merlot, and Syrah. Dry Creek Valley is particularly known for its tracts of old-vine Zinfandel, while Alexander Valley and Knights Valley are better known for their Cabernet Sauvignon and Merlot.
8 **SONOMA VALLEY AVA** 9 **SONOMA MOUNTAIN AVA** 10 **MOON MOUNTAIN AVA**	The large Sonoma Valley appellation comprises a very wide range of climate conditions, ranging from its warmer northern reaches, ideal for ripening stronger red wines, to its cooler southern zones, which are better suited for lighter reds and whites. Sonoma Mountain AVA and Moon Mountain AVA both feature the warmer hillsides sheltered from maritime influence, which favor thick-skinned red grapes, like Cabernet Sauvignon.
11 **CARNEROS AVA**	This unique appellation covers terrain in both Sonoma and Napa counties that is dramatically cooled by San Pablo Bay. It is particularly known for sparkling wines, Chardonnay, and Pinot Noir.

NAPA VALLEY

Vineyards were planted in Napa Valley as early as 1839, but the winemaking trade was slower to bloom here than in neighboring Sonoma. Napa Valley's first commercial winery was founded in 1861 by Charles Krug, who had learned the wine trade by serving as an apprentice to Agoston Haraszthy at Buena Vista. By 1889, there were 140 wineries operating in Napa Valley, but few of them would survive the double whammy of phylloxera and Prohibition in the early twentieth century. It took decades for quality wines to reemerge, but today Napa Valley is the world's most famous AVA and the source of many of California's finest wines.

GEOGRAPHY & CLIMATE

Located farther away from the Pacific, Napa County's climate is warmer. As a result, wine regions located here tend to make stronger, heavier wines from mostly red grapes, which need more sunshine and heat to ripen, like Cabernet Sauvignon, Merlot, Zinfandel, Syrah, and Petite Sirah. Napa Valley is framed by mountains on both sides: its boundary with Sonoma County in the west runs along the Mayacamas range, while the Vaca range to the east separates Napa Valley from the much hotter Sacramento Valley. The main point of ingress for cold air and fog is from San Pablo Bay in the south, so as a rule, Napa Valley's vineyards warm as you travel north. Vines are the most densely planted and easiest to cultivate along the flat valley floor, but in recent years, more vineyards are being planted on its hillside slopes, which are particularly well-suited to growing top-quality grapes for luxury-level wines.

CALIFORNIA'S RED WINE COUNTRY

Until fairly recently, both white and red grapes were cultivated in Napa Valley, but today red grapes greatly outnumber white grapes for a number of reasons. First, most of the region is too warm for growing premium white wines, but it's ideal for robust reds. Second, the American public once preferred white wines, but a greater awareness of the health benefits of moderate consumption of red wines has turned that tide, most notably among top-quality wines.

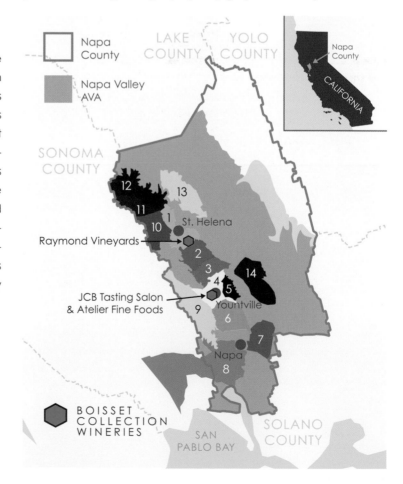

Napa County

Napa Valley AVA

LAKE COUNTY | YOLO COUNTY

Napa County

CALIFORNIA

SONOMA COUNTY

12
13
11
10   1   St. Helena
Raymond Vineyards
2
3   14
4
5
JCB Tasting Salon
& Atelier Fine Foods
Yountville
9
6
7
Napa
8

BOISSET COLLECTION WINERIES

SAN PABLO BAY

SOLANO COUNTY

NAPA VALLEY'S MAIN WINEMAKING ZONES

NAPA VALLEY AVA

Napa County's main AVA fully encompasses all of the sub-appellations listed below (except Carneros—see AVA listing for details). Napa Valley is best known for its red wines, like Cabernet Sauvignon, Merlot, and Zinfandel; however, some Chardonnay and Sauvignon Blanc are grown for white wines.

1 **ST. HELENA AVA**
2 **RUTHERFORD AVA**
3 **OAKVILLE AVA**
4 **YOUNTVILLE AVA**
5 **STAG'S LEAP DISTRICT AVA**

These five AVAs form the heart of Napa Valley wine country. The AVAs of St. Helena, Rutherford, Oakville and Yountville encompass the original valley floor and benchland vineyards that first brought renown to Napa Valley's Cabernet Sauvignon and Merlot wines. Stag's Leap District AVA is a hillier zone, where the valley floor transitions into the Vaca range of mountains to the east, but is also a stronghold for Cabernet Sauvignon and Merlot.

6 **OAK KNOLL DISTRICT AVA**
7 **COOMBSVILLE AVA**

Surrounding the city of Napa in the south, these AVAs are quite cool thanks to the nearby bay. Their higher, warmer hillside sites are known for Cabernet Sauvignon, while their lower, cooler vineyards may grow varieties like Chardonnay.

8 **LOS CARNEROS AVA**

The Los Carneros AVA covers lower elevations closer to the cooling influence of San Pablo Bay. It is shared with Sonoma County and is best known for sparkling wines, Chardonnay, and Pinot Noir.

9 **MOUNT VEEDER AVA**
10 **SPRING MOUNTAIN AVA**
11 **DIAMOND MOUNTAIN AVA**

These 3 AVAs are all located in the hills above the valley floor in the Mayacamas mountains, which separate Napa Valley from Sonoma County. Mount Veeder AVA is the coolest, being closest to San Pablo Bay. Spring Mountain and Diamond Mountain AVAs are both warmer and more sheltered. All three appellations are known primarily for their excellent Cabernet Sauvignon.

12 **CALISTOGA AVA**

Located in the valley's northwestern corner, Calistoga AVA comprises mainly valley floor vineyard sites and is adjacent to Sonoma's Knights Valley AVA. This region is the warmest of Napa Valley's growing regions and favors grapes like Cabernet Sauvignon and Zinfandel.

13 **HOWELL MOUNTAIN AVA**
14 **ATLAS PEAK AVA**

These two AVAs are located above the valley floor in the hills of the Vaca mountains, which form Napa Valley's eastern boundary. Howell Mountain AVA covers prestige hillside sites and is renowned for its fine Cabernet Sauvignon. Atlas Peak AVA is considerably cooler, a remote valley known for Cabernet Sauvignon, Merlot, and Sangiovese.

GLOSSARY

Acidic, Acidity   Detectable presence of sourness; one of the six true taste sensations detected by the tongue's taste buds.

Age-worthy   A descriptive term for wines that resist oxidation, thanks to high levels of natural preservative components like tannins or acidity.

Alcohol   Ethanol, the psychoactive component in adult beverages like wine; an organic compound derived from sugar by the metabolism of living yeast cultures.

Antioxidant   A substance that inhibits oxidation or its properties, as with phenolic compounds in grape skins (i.e., tannins).

Apéritif   Alcoholic drink designed to pique the appetite before a meal. Note, however, that while lightweight wines are frequently served in an apéritif role, the term "apéritif wine" may also refer to a category of flavored and fortified wine-based drinks that are typically sold as spirits. All vermouths are "apéritif wines," for example, as are Lillet and Dubonnet.

Appellation   A formal region-of-origin statement, indicating where a wine's grapes were grown; mandatory on all wine labels.

Archetype   Original specimen or pattern on which subsequent examples are modeled.

Aromatics   Wine components perceived by the sense of smell that convey sensations of both scent and flavor.

Astringency   In wine, the mouth-drying effect of tannins found in grape skins, which suppresses salivation.

Barrel   Round storage vessels made of oak, used in the maturation or fermentation of wine.

Barrel-Aging   A common practice in red winemaking, where young, fresh wines are stored in oak barrels after fermentation for anywhere from a few weeks to a few years.

Barrel-Fermentation   A white winemaking practice where grape juice is fermented into wines in oak barrels; these wines are often aged on their yeast sediments for up to a year.

Barrique   Traditional small French-style wine barrel; associated with styles where new oak flavor is imparted during aging; typically contains 225-230L of wine.

Biodynamic   A form of natural farming designed to maintain the health of the vineyard's inter-related ecosystem (which includes the soil, plants, and animals); a rigorous agricultural certification system that prohibits the use of non-native and synthetic treatments and organizes cultivation around the lunar cycle.

Bitter, Bitterness   In sensory science, one of the six sensations detected by the tongue's taste buds (e.g., hops in beer); often confused with the tactile astringency of tannins (e.g., in wine and black tea).

Blend   A wine made by combining different grape varieties, which may be mixed before fermentation, after fermentation, or after maturation (at the point of bottling).

Body   Descriptive term for wine's texture, typically driven by alcohol content. See "Weight."

Bold   Descriptive term for wine that is high in aromatic compounds and, therefore, flavor intensity; concentrated.

Brand Name   A wine's commercial identity; may be the vintner's name or the proprietary name for a product line.

Browning   In wine, a visible sign of oxidation and age. In food, the color change associated with caramelization and Maillard reactions in certain cooking methods, like searing, frying, and grilling.

Brut   Regulated label term for sparkling wines that have no perceptible sweetness; one step drier than "Extra Dry."

Bulk Wine   The lowest quality category of wines, often used in cheap blends.

Carbonated   Descriptive term for wine that is bubbly, releasing spontaneous bubbles of carbon dioxide when opened.

Cellaring   Bottle-aging; maturing of wine by purchasers after its commercial release.

Color Compounds   Phenolic wine components, like tannins, that are derived from grape skins and that give red and rosé wines color and flavor.

Complex   Wine term for multiple simultaneous sensations in wine; typically refers to the presence of many pleasing scents and flavors, especially those generated during fermentation or aging.

Concentrated   Descriptive term for wines with higher-than-average intensity of olfactory scents and flavors; typically refers to fruit rather than oak.

Cork Taint, Corked   Detectable spoilage of wine caused by contact with natural cork; most commonly the presence of TCA (short for 2,4,6-trichloroanisole), a compound that gives wine an unpleasant mildewy smell.

Corks   Wooden wine bottle stoppers punched from the bark of the cork oak tree. Most of the world's cork is grown in Portugal and Spain.

Crisp   Descriptive term for wines that have a standard, moderate "tangy" level of acidity.

Cru   A French wine term used for recognizing sites that produce superior wines, typically qualified as top-level *Grand Cru* or next-best *Premier Cru*. Often translated as "growth," its meaning is closer to "rank" and is complicated by different criteria in different regions that are enforced with varying rigor.

Cuvée, Cuvée Name   Wine term for a particular bottling of wine, often needed to distinguish when more than one wine is made in the same appellation and from the same grape; from the French word for "vat." In some regions, a narrower usage that indicates a blended wine.

Decanting, Decanter   Process or container used for removing wine from its bottle before it is served, either to separate an older red wine from its sediment or to aerate a younger wine.

Démi-Sec   Regulated French label term for wines with overt sweetness; these are typically balanced, "sweet-tart" wines.

Dessert Wine   A category of wines that feature overt, intense sweetness.

Distilled Spirits   High-alcohol beverages, like brandy and whiskey; made from low-alcohol fermented products, like wine and beer, by vaporizing their alcohol and re-condensing it in a separate container.

Dry, Dryness   Descriptive term for wine with no noticeable presence of sugar; the opposite of sweet and the norm for the majority of wines. Easily confused with the mouth-drying effect of tannins in red wines.

Earthy   Descriptive term for wine with aromas reminiscent of the outdoors and farm environments, such as mushrooms, root vegetables, mulch, stones, or fallen leaves.

Estate   A vineyard owned by the vintner who makes its wine, allowing them to farm their own grapes rather than purchasing from a grower (the latter is the norm).

Estate-Bottled   Regulated label term used primarily for New World wines, indicating that the vintner owns and farms the vineyard from whose grapes a wine was made.

Esters   Volatile aromatic compounds that are a major source of scent and flavor in many fruits and in wine.

Everyday Wine   Simple wines that are fairly priced; a step above bulk wines and the cheapest of the fine wines.

Extra-Dry   Regulated label term for sparkling wines that have faint perceptible sweetness; one step sweeter than "Brut."

Fermentation   Main stage of winemaking, which converts juice into wine; the process by which all alcoholic drinks are made, where living yeast organisms consume and metabolize sugar, breaking it down into alcohol and carbon dioxide.

Fine Wine   Premium wines where quality is a consideration.

Finish   Wine term for wine's aftertaste; a desirable trait that is useful for assessing wine quality; measured by its duration.

Flabby   Descriptive term for wine that has lower-than-average levels of acidity.

Flavor   In common usage, taste sensations derived from eating and drinking; for purposes of wine analysis, aromas that reach the olfactory nerves from the mouth internally via the retro-nasal passage.

Food-Friendly, Food-Oriented   Wine term for wines designed to taste best with food, especially the acid-blocking, fruit-enhancing effects of salt in food.

Fortified Wine   Category of wines ranging from 15% to 20% alcohol that contain added distilled spirits, such as Port and Sherry.

Freeze-Concentrate   Reducing the water content of a liquid by freezing it and removing its solid ice crystals. See "Ice Wine."

Fruit, Fruity   In common usage, sweet edible produce, typically containing seeds of a flowering plant. In wine tasting, a descriptive term for wine aromas derived from grapes or the winemaking process; when prominent, wine may be described as "fruity," "fruit-driven," or "fruit-forward."

Full-Bodied   Wine term for wines of richer-than-average texture. See "Heavy."

Generic   Common or nonexclusive. In New World wines, refers to wines that do not specify a grape variety on their label. In Old World wines, refers to the most basic wines of a region (e.g., generic Bourgogne as opposed to a wine from a superior subdistrict of Burgundy).

Grand Cru   A French wine quality classification. See "Cru."

Grape Variety   Cultivar of the grape species *vitis vinifera*; includes the many types of grapes used in winemaking.

Green   In fruit, underripe; in wine, displaying characteristics associated with low ripeness, such as high acidity and leafy, herbal aromatics.

Grip   Descriptive term for the astringent, mouth-drying tactile sensation of the tannins found in many red wines.

Harsh   Descriptive term for a strong presence of either an astringent, mouth-drying sensation of tannins in red wine or an unusually high alcohol level in any wine.

Headspace   The upper section of a wine glass bowl that remains empty to allow swirling and to concentrate wine aromas.

Heavy   Descriptive term for wines with a rich, mouth-coating texture; associated with wines containing over 14% alcohol.

Herbal   Descriptive term for wines whose aromas and flavors resemble herbs, leaves, or vegetables.

Ice Wine   A dessert wine style made by freeze-concentrating the juice, often by harvesting frozen grapes in midwinter.

Indigenous   Originating from a particular region.

Jammy   Descriptive term for wines whose aromas and flavors suggest fruit that has been cooked or sweetened.

Lactone   Aromatic ester found in oak barrels, which contributes to the "oaky" flavor in wine.

Late-Harvest   Label term used for sweet wines, referencing the technique of allowing the fruit to hang longer on the vine to become sweeter and more ripe.

Legs   The drips that form when wine is swirled in a glass; a visible indicator of high levels of either alcohol or sugar or both.

Length   See "Finish."

Light, Lightweight   Descriptive term for wines with a sheer, delicate texture; associated with wines containing below 13% alcohol.

Madeirization   Flavor changes in wine caused by exposure to heat; named for the wines of Madeira.

Maturation, Mature   Winemaking stage where wine rests in barrels, tanks, or bottles after fermentation; descriptive term for wine at its peak that requires no further aging.

Midweight   Descriptive term for wines with moderate texture, neither light nor heavy; associated with wines containing between 13% and 14% alcohol.

Mild   Descriptive term for wine that is low in aromatic or flavor intensity.

Mousse   Descriptive term for the carbonation of wine.

Mouth-Drying   See "Tannic."

Mouthfeel   Tactile sensations of food and drink perceived in the mouth.

Naked   See "Unoaked."

Neutral Barrel   An oak barrel that has been used to store wine for at least three years, reducing its ability to impart "new oak" flavors.

New Oak   Oak barrels or products that have not previously come into contact with wine; also, the flavors and scents that these impart.

New World   Collective term for the wine regions of the Americas and the southern hemisphere.

Oak, Oaky   In common usage, a type of tree or its wood. In wine tasting, a descriptive term for a category of wine aromas that are derived from the wine's contact with new oak barrels or oak flavoring agents during winemaking.

Oaked   Category of wines given contact with new oak barrels or oak flavoring agents during winemaking, or the process of imparting oak flavor through barrel-aging or barrel-fermentation.

Off-Dry   Lightly sweet; not fully dry.

Old World   Wine term for traditional wine regions of Europe.

Olfactory   Of or relating to the sense of smell.

Organic   Type of natural farming and the agricultural certification of products that prohibits the use of synthetic chemical treatments.

Oxidation, Oxidized   The primary source of wine spoilage resulting from prolonged exposure to air, typically avoided during winemaking; a descriptive term for its effects on wine, such as reduced freshness, browned color, and nutty "cooked" fruit aromas.

Pairing   Choosing a wine for its suitability as a flattering partner for a particular food item.

Palate   Technically, the soft flesh of the mouth; also used informally to refer to a person's sensitivity to tastes and smells or to a person's wine preferences.

Phenolic Compounds   Color and flavor compounds found in grape skins, like tannins and anthocyanins; many are antioxidants with natural preservative properties.

Potential Alcohol   Sugar content of grapes prior to fermentation, which by definition defines the upper limit of the alcoholic content of wine made from them.

Premier Cru   A French wine quality classification. See "Cru."

Preservative   A substance that slows spoilage and oxidation; may be naturally present in wine (as with tannins) or may be an additive (such as sulfur dioxide).

Proprietary Name   A wine name that is particular to a specific vintner, as with a cuvée name or brand name.

Racy   Descriptive term for wine that has high levels of acidity.

Refreshing   Descriptive term for wines whose acidity provides a bracing, restorative sensation.

Reserve, Reserva, Riserva   Wine label terms that suggest superior quality; regulated in Spain, Italy, and South America but with no legal standards elsewhere.

Rich   Descriptive term for wines that feel more thick or viscous in the mouth than average. See "Heavy."

Ripeness   Final stage of fruit development during final weeks before harvest, when exposure to sunlight and warmth causes grapes to become sweet, juicy, and ready to pick.

Rosé   Category of wines that are pink in color, made by giving clear grape juice brief contact with dark grape skins during winemaking.

Saccharomyces   The genus of "sugar-eating" yeasts that produce beverage alcohol; the category used for making wine, beer, and bread.

Salt, Saltiness   A common food component that reduces the perceived acidity of wine when served alongside it; one of the six true taste sensations detected by the tongue's taste buds.

Sediment   A solid precipitate that settles from a liquid.

Sensory   Of or relating to perceptions of sight, smell, taste, touch, and hearing.

Sharp   Descriptive term for wines that have a high "tart" level of acidity.

Single Vineyard   Wine made from grapes grown on one plot of land.

Soft   Descriptive term for wines that are low in astringent tannins; also sometimes applied to low-acid wines.

Sommelier   Wine steward or wine-specific server in a restaurant; typically also in charge of wine purchasing.

Sour   See "Acidic."

Sparkling   Descriptive term for carbonated wine with bubbles.

Spritzy   Descriptive term for faintly carbonated wine.

Stainless Steel   Material used in most modern fermentation vessels; in white wines, a descriptive term for an unoaked style.

Still   Descriptive term for wine that has no carbonation or bubbles.

Strength   Descriptive term for wine's alcoholic content; wines over 13.5% alcohol are considered "strong," while those below this mark are considered "light."

Subtle   Descriptive term for wines with lower-than-average intensity of olfactory scents and flavors. See "Mild."

Sweet, Sweetness   Detectable presence of sugar; one of the six true taste sensations detected by the tongue's taste buds.

Table Grapes   Grapes grown for use as fresh produce; often seedless, juicy, and thin-skinned.

Tactile   Of or relating to the sense of touch.

Tannin, Tannic   Phenolic compound with astringent properties found in grape skins, which acts as a natural preservative; the drying feeling it leaves in the mouth after tasting red wines.

Taste, Tasting   In common usage, all sensations derived from eating or drinking or the activity of sampling food or drink; for purposes of wine analysis, the only one of the six sensations detectable with the tongue's taste buds.

Taste Buds   Clusters of nerves scattered across the tongue; the mechanism for perceiving taste sensations.

Tears   The drips that form when wine is swirled in a glass. See "Legs."

Temperate   Climate category suitable for growing grapes; neither too cold in the winter nor too hot and tropical.

Terpene   Type of aromatic compound responsible for intense floral scents in grapes like Moscato, Gewurztraminer, and Riesling.

Terroir   Wine term for location-specific sensory characteristics in wine, often distinctive earthy aromas associated with a particular region or vineyard; may also refer to the unique aspects of a region or a vineyard's geography that create these traits.

Texture   Descriptive term for wine's body or viscosity, typically driven by alcoholic content. See "Weight."

Toasty, Toasted   Descriptive terms for wine with oak smells; nutty, caramelized scents and flavors derived from the flame "toasting" of wood during barrel-making.

Umami   One of the six sensations detected by the tongue's taste buds; an overall "yummy" taste caused by glutamates and amino acids.

Unoaked   Descriptive term for wines that do not come into contact with oak or barrels in winemaking, or whose flavor and scent feature no detectable presence of new oak.

Unwooded   See "Unoaked."

Vanillin   Principal flavor compound of vanilla beans, also strongly present in oak and a major contributor of the "oaky" flavors in wine.

Vin Doux Naturel   Type of French dessert wines made by mutage, or the "Port Method" of fortification.

Vintage   The year in which a wine's grapes were harvested; often included on wine labels.

Vintner   Producer of wine.

Viscosity   Texture or thickness in a liquid. See "Weight."

Vitis Vinifera   Primary species of grapevine used for winemaking; of Eurasian origin.

Volatile   Evaporates readily at normal temperatures; a characteristic of many wine components, particularly alcohol and flavor compounds like esters.

Weight   Descriptive term for wine's texture, perceived as thickness or viscosity in the mouth. Wines with more alcohol or lots of sugar feel "heavier" than those that are lower in alcohol and/or drier.

Winemaking   The process of transforming fresh grapes into wine through fermentation.

Workhorse Grape   A grape variety capable of making pleasant wines even at very high yields; often used for bulk wines and bargain wines.

Yeast   Single-celled microscopic organisms that convert sugar into alcohol; agent of fermentation essential for winemaking.

Yield   Measure of vineyard productivity, typically in tons of grapes per acre or hectoliters of juice per hectare.

Young   Descriptive term for wine that is not barrel-aged before release or bottle-aged thereafter; typically applied to wines that are less than two years old.

INDEX

DEDICATION

To my grandparents—schoolteachers all—who instilled in me a love of learning, and to my parents and parents-in-law, for my passion for life.

To my sister for her guidance, my wife, Gina, for being my muse, and my ladies, as I call my daughters, for being my illumination.

And to all of our ambassadors and wine lovers for their thirst for knowledge of the world of wine at large; you inspired this book.

ACKNOWLEDGMENTS

A number of people helped bring this book to life. We would like to extend our thanks and deepest appreciation to:

Sheila Thomas, Kristin Connelly, Mary Velgos, Vicky Shea, and the team at Southwestern Publishing Group, Inc., for their expertise and excellent work.

Amberly Austad and the design team at Lemonly for their brilliant executions of our infographics and visual explanations.

Patrick Egan at Boisset Collection for shepherding the project and illuminating Jean-Charles' vision and writing to come alive on the pages of this book, as well as Nicole Rosenstiel, Mira Coburn, and the entire Boisset Collection family for their efforts in sourcing images and providing design direction.

The Bourgogne Wine Board (BIVB), Napa Valley Vintners Association (NVV), and Sonoma County Vintners for their excellent educational resources.

Clare Pelino and Robert Bednarz for the referrals and introductions that helped get this project off the ground.

We would also like to thank the following companies and organizations that have generously given permission for us to include images of properties or their products: Baccarat, Robert Mondavi Winery, and the University of Pennsylvania Museum of Archaeology and Anthropology.

BOISSET
Collection

Favorite Recipes® Press

Boisset is a family-owned collection of historic and unique wineries bound together by a common cause: authentic, terroir-driven wines in harmony with their history, their future, and the land and people essential to their existence. With more than twenty historical and prestigious wineries in the world's preeminent terroirs, including the Côte d'Or, Beaujolais, Rhône Valley, California's Russian River Valley, and the Napa Valley, each house retains its unique history, identity, and style, and all are united in the pursuit of fine wines expressive of their terroir.

Boisset Collection
849 Zinfandel Lane
St. Helena, CA 94574
BoissetCollection.com

ISBN: 978-0-87197-646-8
Library of Congress Catalog Number: 2017963116
Printed in China
10 9 8 7 6 5 4 3 2 1

Passion For Wine was edited, designed, and manufactured by Favorite Recipes Press in collaboration with Boisset Collection. Favorite Recipes Press works with top chefs, food and appliance manufacturers, restaurants and resorts, health organizations, Junior Leagues, and nonprofit organizations to create award-winning cookbooks and other food-related products. Favorite Recipes Press is an imprint of Southwestern Publishing Group, Inc., 2451 Atrium Way, Nashville, Tennessee 37214. Southwestern Publishing Group is a wholly owned subsidiary of Southwestern/Great American, Inc., Nashville, Tennessee.

Christopher G. Capen, President, Southwestern
    Publishing Group
Sheila Thomas, President and Publisher, Favorite
    Recipes Press
Mary Velgos, Jacket and Interior Designer
Vicky Shea, Senior Art Director
Kristin Connelly, Managing Editor
Lisa Howard, Copy Editor
Linda Brock, Proofreader
Lemonly, Infographic Illustrations

www.frpbooks.com | 800-358-0560

Cover photograph © Alexander Rubin